Creole Made Easy Workbook

With Expanded Guide and Practical Lessons

- Expanded explanations for the *Creole Made Easy* textbook lessons
- Practice worksheets with key for each chapter
- Final exam and key
- Additional bonus chapters with applied Creole and practical lessons including:
  - Numbers and Time
  - Months, Days, Seasons, and Weather
  - Colors
  - Family and Friends
  - Marketplace and Food
  - Around the House
  - Health and Medicine
- 180 pages of must have information

Betty J. Turnbull

Light Messages
5216 Tahoe Drive
Durham, NC 27713 U.S.A.
creole@lightmessages.com
www.lightmessages.com

Copyright © 2005 by Light Messages

First Printing May 2005

International Standard Book Number: 0-9679937-7-6

Printed in the United States of America

Table of Contents

Lesson One
Pronunciation and Word Order

Mastering the sounds of the Creole vowels is key to learning the language. The more natural the sounds become the easier understanding, speaking and writing the Creole language will be. While the first three lessons may seem short and easy, make sure that you are comfortable with the sounds before continuing.

Practice saying these vowel sounds. The vowel sounds are repeated in random order in the chart below. Repeat and memorize the Creole sounds (using the English vowel sound in the key word as a guide):

Creole	English key	Creole	English key
a	o in lot	o	abbreviated o in go
e	a in day	ou	ou in soup
è	e in let	e	a in day
i	the double ee in seed	ay	i in ice
o	abbreviated o in go	i	the double ee in seed
ò	o in or	è	e in let
ay	i in ice	ò	o in or
ou	ou in soup	a	o in lot
è	e in let	i	the double ee in seed
a	o in lot	ay	i in ice
i	the double ee in seed	o	abbreviated o in go
ou	ou in soup	a	o in lot
o	abbreviated o in go	ou	ou in soup
e	a in day	ò	o in or
ay	i in ice	e	a in day
ò	o in or	è	e in let

When you think you know the sounds, try covering the English key. Now say each sound from memory. Make a set of flash cards for each lesson as you go along. This can be done with 3 x 5 index cards. Write the Creole word or sound on one side and the English equivalent on the other. Keep these cards handy and use them at the beginning of each new lesson. This is like using a pitch pipe in music before starting. It will help put your mind into Creole "gear" before learning something new.

While it is true that the letter **u** is not used alone but is used in combination with **o** as in **ou**, there is one exception to this rule. The number **eight** is **uit**. Pronounce **uit** by saying **you eat**. Now say it very quickly, shortening each word until they run together and almost sound like one word. (This applies to other forms of eight, such as eighty, eighteen, as well.)

Memorize the vocabulary using the sounds learned. Use the flash cards between studying lessons for review.

With the vocabulary provided in this lesson you are now ready to form your first Creole sentences. The order of words in a Creole sentence is very similar to that of English with a couple of exceptions. The subject, verb, and object pattern is the same. The exceptions include the article *the*, which comes after the noun and possessive pronouns. This is covered in more depth in lesson 4. Possessive pronouns also come after the noun. This is covered in lesson 5.

Read the English and substitute the Creole word in place of each English word. Try this sentence:

You – **ou**, *can* – **kapab**, *give* – **bay**.
Ou kapab bay. *You can give.*

The Creole word **bay** (*give*) changes forms when used with a pronoun. (This is an exception to most Creole words.) When using **li** *(he* or *she)*, **ou** and **yo**, **bay** becomes **ba** <u>when used before pronouns.</u> It is important to understand that the pronunciation also changes. The **y** is no longer present, so is not pronounced. The word is pronounced **b** (*b* as in ball) **a** (the *o* sound of lot).

When **bay** is being used to mean *to deliver* (instead of give) with **li** as an object, it does not change. **Ki kote pou mwen bay li** – *Where do I deliver (give) it.*

You can give one - **Ou kapab bay youn.**
You can give him one – **Ou kapab ba li youn.**

Bay becomes **ban** <u>when used before the pronouns</u> *mwen* and *nou*. Again, note the change in pronunciation. The *an* sound is covered in Lesson 2, but we will briefly go over it here. The sound *an* in Creole is a nasalized sound much like the *un* in bunny. To nasalize the sound, push the *un* sound through your nose (See Lesson 2). So **ban** becomes **b** (*b* as in ball) and **an** (*un* sound of bunny).

The above rules are only true when **bay** is used before the pronoun.

Bay mwen bagay la becomes **ban mwen bagay la**. (*Give me the thing.*)

Mwen bay bagay la remains the same (*I give the thing.*)

Continue with the other sentences. When you have completed these, review your sounds and vocabulary and do the worksheet for lesson one. Continue to Lesson 2.

Note:

The word **kapab** can be contracted to **ka** or **kab**. When in doubt **kapab** will always be understood.

Ou kapab bay could be said as:

Ou ka bay. Since **bay** begins with a **b** you would not say **kab**.

(The use of contractions is covered in greater detail in Lesson 8.)

Worksheet Lesson One

Write the Creole word in the blank:

the thing	_____	yes	_____
little	_____	not	_____
person	_____	page	_____
there	_____	can	_____

Fill in the blank:

1. Ou _____ ba yo li.
   You can give them it.

2. Ban _____ ti bagay la.
   Give us the little thing.

3. Wi, yo kapab ba _____ li.
   Yes, they can give you it.

4. _____ nou li.
   Give us it. (Give it to us.)

1. Bay li _____
   Give it there.

Write the phrase below using the correct form of "give"

Give it _____

Give him_____

They give _____

She gives_____

Give them _____

Give us_____

We give you_____

They give them _____

She gives him _____

You give us _____

Draw a line to connect the two words that mean the same thing:

little   bagay la
page   kapab
someone   nou
can   wi
the thing   paj
us   pa
she   li
yes   pou
not   piti
for   yon moun

Translate the sentence:

Li ba li bagay la.

_____

Key Worksheet Lesson One

Write the Creole word in the blank:

the thing	*bagay la*	yes	*wi*
little	*piti, ti*	not	*pa*
person	*moun*	page	*paj*
there	*la*	can	*kapab, ka, kab*

Fill in the blank:

1. Ou __*kapab*__ ba yo li.
   You can give them it.
2. Ban _*nou*_ ti bagay la.
   Give us the little thing.
3. Wi, yo kapab ba <u>*ou*</u> li.
   Yes, they can give you it.
4. <u>*Ban*</u> nou li.
   Give us it. (Give it to us.)
2. Bay li _*la*_
   Give it there.

Write the phrase below using the correct form of *give*
Give it... <u>*Bay li...*</u>
Give him – <u>*Ba li*</u>
They give... <u>*Yo bay...*</u>
She gives... <u>*Li bay...*</u>
Give them... <u>*Ba yo*</u>
Give us... <u>*Ban nou...*</u>
We give you... <u>*Nou ba ou...*</u>
They give them... <u>*Yo ba yo...*</u>
She gives him... <u>*Li ba li...*</u>
You give us... <u>*Ou ban nou...*</u>

Draw a line to connect the two words that mean the same thing:

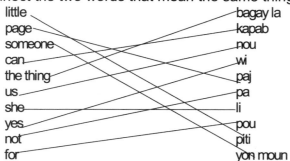

little	bagay la
page	kapab
someone	nou
can	wi
the thing	paj
us	pa
she	li
yes	pou
not	piti
for	yon moun

Translate the sentence:
Li ba li bagay la.

<u>*He gives him the thing.*</u>

Lesson Two
Pronunciation – Nasal Sounds

Begin this lesson by reviewing the sounds of the vowels from Lesson One. Using the flash cards, practice saying the vowel sounds. Next review the vocabulary from Lesson One.

Making the nasal sounds in Creole is not very difficult. You can make these sounds by saying the letters while holding your nose and "pushing" the sound through your nose.

Consider the letter combinations of **an, en** and **on** in Creole as their own letters, ones not contained in the English language. The letter **an** in Creole sounds closest to the *un* in **bunny**. Say *un*. Now push the sound through your nose. Now repeat the sound, but stop short of actually pronouncing the *n*. The *n* of the *un* in bunny is silent, yet it influences the way the *u* is pronounced. Practice saying **an** by holding your nose and making it sound like the *u* in bunny, but nasalized. Now try it by pushing the sound through your nose without actually holding the nose.

The **en** sound in Creole is like the *en* in **enjoy**. In Creole, the *n* is not pronounced but does influence how the *e* is pronounced. Practice saying enjoy by holding your nose and "pushing" the sound through. Now say the *e* of that sound several times while holding your nose. Practice making the same sound without holding your nose.

The letter **on** sounds most like the *on* sound of **don't**. Again the **n** is not pronounced, but does influence how the *o* sounds. Practice this sound as you did the others, while holding you nose and then reproducing the sound without holding your nose. Remember to "push" the sounds through the nose.

Each letter of a word is pronounced in Creole. Remember that the pairs **an, en** and **on** are considered three letters of the Creole language, so do not be confused by the above statement "the *n* is silent." While the *n* does not sound like an English spoken *n* it is still being pronounced as the compound letter **an, en** or **on**.

Note that when a word has **an**, followed by **n** as in **tann** (wait for), the first n is a part of the letter **an** and is not pronounced as the English sound *n*, but the second **n** is pronounced. **Tann** is made up of three letters or sounds; **t – an – n**. Say this word by saying a **t** sound, the nasalized **an** and then the **n** sound. Practice saying this.

Bonus vocabulary using nasal sounds:

fish	pwason	cookie	bonbon
chin	manton	bread	pen
song	chan	path, trail	chemen

Vocabulary Note: *Here* is translated as **isit la** when meaning a location and **isit** when referring to presence. Sometimes the **t** of **isit** is dropped. If so, **isit la** becomes **isi a**. It is always correct ot use **isit** and **isit la**.

Everyone is here - **Tout moun isit - Tout moun isi**
The house is here – **Kay la isit la - Kay la isi a**
Give it here – **Ba li isit la - Ba li isi a**

However, when *here* is used before a noun or pronoun it is translated as **men**.

Here I am – **Men mwen**
Here it is – **Men li**
Here is the house – **Men kay la**

Add the sound flash cards for this lesson to the sound flash cards in lesson one. Try saying each sound several times; mixing the cards so you do them in a different order each time.

Memorize the vocabulary using the sounds learned. Proceed to the worksheet for this lesson.

Worksheet Lesson Two

Write the Creole word in the blank:

to take	_____	many	_____
work	_____	here	_____
lime	_____	soap	_____
wait for	_____	good	_____
slowly	_____	happy	_____
three	_____	in	_____

Fill in the blank:

1. Jan _____ ou la.
   John waits for you there.

2. _____ twa sitwon.
   Take three limes.

3. Ba li _____.
   Give her the peanut butter.

4. Pran li _____.
   Take it slowly.

5. Li ba yo _____ savon.
   He gives them much soap.

Write the Creole sentence.

Give him the load. _____

Wait for them there. _____

Do not take three limes._____

Give John the good peanut butter. _____

You wait for us here. _____

He works slowly. _____

Give it in the house._____

Do not wait for him there. _____

Here is the house. _____

Choose the correct word and write it under the picture:

pen, pwason, manton, chemen, chan, bonbon

_____

_____

_____

_____

_____

_____

Key Lesson Two Worksheet

Write the Creole word in the blank:

to take	*pran*	many	*anpil*
work	*travay*	here	*isit la*
lime	*sitwon*	soap	*savon*
wait for	*tann*	good	*bon*
slowly	*dousman*	happy	*kontan*
three	*twa*	in	*nan*

Fill in the blank:
1. Jan _*tann*_ ou la.
   John waits for you there.
2. _*Pran*_ twa sitwon.
   Take three limes.
3. Ba li _*manba a*_ .
   Give her the peanut butter.
4. Pran li _*dousman*_ .
   Take it slowly.
5. Li ba yo _*anpil*_ savon.
   He gives them much soap.

Write the Creole sentence.

Give him the load. _Ba li chajman an._
Wait for them there. _Tann yo la._
Do not take three limes. _Pa pran twa sitwon._
Give John the good peanut butter. _Bay Jan bon manba a_.
You wait for us here. _Ou tann nou isit la._
He works slowly. _Li travay dousman_.
Give it in the house. _Ba li nan kay la_.
Do not wait for him there. _Pa tann li la_.
Here is the house. _Men kay la._

chemen

bonbon

pwason

manton

pen

chan

Lesson Three
Pronunciation

Begin this lesson by reviewing the sounds of the vowels from the first two lessons. Using the flash cards, practice saying each sound. Next review the vocabulary from lessons one and two.

As is stated in the lesson, most consonants are pronounced the same in Creole as in English. Remember that in Creole each letter is pronounced. The letters **c** and **h** do not appear in the Creole as stand alone letters. They are used only in combination together, **ch**, which can be taken as one letter.

Repeat the following sounds:

ch as in **sh** of **sh**ip
g as in **g** of **g**o
j as in **s** of mea**s**ure
s as in **s** of **s**oft
w as in **w** of **w**in
y as in **y** of **y**es

> Memorize the sounds of **ch**, **g**, **j**, **s**, **w**, and **y**. Make and add these flash cards to the ones you are already using and practice the different sounds until you are comfortable with them and know them all without having to review.

Vocabulary Note: *With* is translated as **avèk**, frequently shortened to **ak**. They are often used interchangeably, however, there is a rule which determines when **ak** is correct. **Avèk** can mean both *with (using)* and *with (accompanied by)* and is always correct. While **ak** is only used when expressing *with*, meaning *accompanied by*.

They are coming with him – **Yo ap vini avèk li** or **Yo ap vini ak li**
I come with him – **Mwen vini avèk li** or **Mwen vini ak li**.

Light it with a match – **Limen li avèk yon alimèt**
I make a cake with two eggs – **Mwen fè yon gato avèk de ze**

Memorize the vocabulary using the sounds learned and do the exercises.

CONGRATULATIONS! With the completion of Lesson Three you are well on your way to speaking Creole. Once you have mastered the sounds, you only need vocabulary to build on your ability to make simple sentences. To prove this, take a look at sentence 8 in Exercise 3. You are making a compound sentence and expressing two thoughts yet you are only on the third lesson!

We reside in the small house, but we cannot do the work well there.
Nou rete nan ti kay la, men nou pa kapab fè travay la byen la.

After you have completed the Lesson Three worksheet you may continue to the next lesson. You have no more pronunciation to learn (only to review), so now it's time to build up your vocabulary.

To help prepare you for the next lesson, learn each lesson's vocabulary words before doing the lesson. Make and use flash cards for the consonant sounds above and add them to your vocabulary flash cards. Proceed to the worksheet for this lesson.

Worksheet Lesson Three

Write the Creole word in the blank:

to need	_____	behind	_____
stop	_____	dog	_____
basket	_____	but	_____
first	_____	with	_____
me, I	_____	want	_____
well	_____	far	_____
have	_____	some	_____

Fill in the blank:

1. Li _____ la.
   He stops there.

2. Mwen _____ twa _____.
   I have three dogs.

3. _____ chajman an avèk mwen.
   Pull the load with me.

4. Yo travay _____.
   They work well.

3. Mwen _____ anpil travay.
   I have much work.

Write the Creole sentence.

Take four limes. _____

They want to pull the load. _____

I have four baskets. _____

He works well but slowly. _____

She waits for you here. _____

She has some beautiful baskets. _____

Yes, you can stop there. _____

I want the peanut butter. _____

They do three lessons well. _____

Choose the word that best describes the picture and write its letter next to the picture.

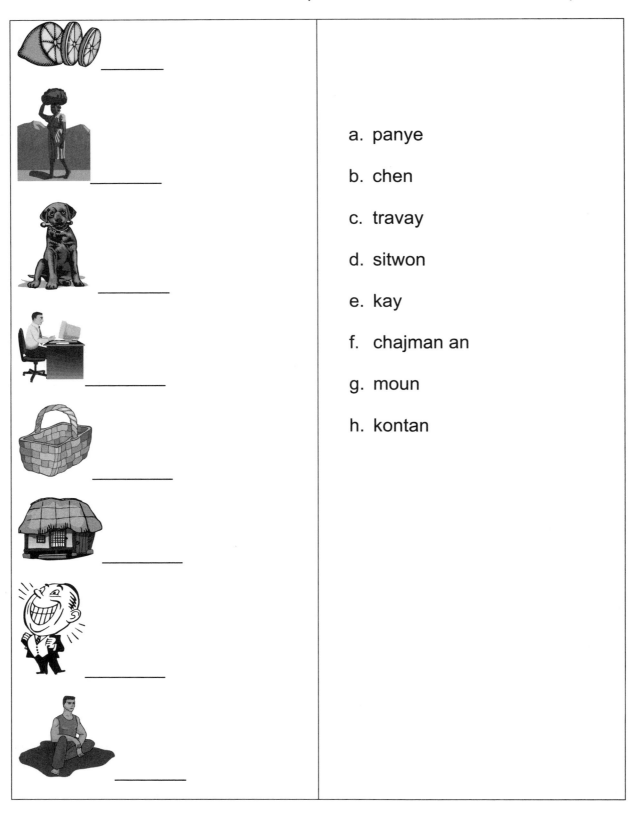

a. panye

b. chen

c. travay

d. sitwon

e. kay

f. chajman an

g. moun

h. kontan

Find the sentence that goes with the picture and write it beneath the picture.

Mwen genyen yon chen.

Li kontan.

Ou travay byen.

_____   _____   _____

Key Worksheet Lesson Three

Write the Creole word in the blank"

to need	*bezwen*	behind	*dèyè*
stop	*rete*	dog	*chen*
basket	*panye*	but	*men*
first	*premye*	with	*avèk*
me, I	*mwen*	want	*vle*
well	*byen*	far	*lwen*
have	*genyen*	some	*kèk*

Fill in the blank:

1. Li _*rete*_ la.
   He stops there.

2. Mwen _*genyen*_ twa _*chen*_.
   I have three dogs.

3. _*Rale*_ chajman an avèk mwen.
   Pull the load with me.

4. Yo travay _*byen*_.
   They work well.

4. Mwen _*genyen*_ anpil travay.
   I have much work.

Write the Creole sentence.

Take four limes. _*Pran kat sitwon*_.

They want to pull the load. _*Yo vle rale chajman an.*_

I have four baskets. _*Mwen genyen kat panye.*_

He works well but slowly. _*Li travay byen men dousman*_.

She waits for you here. _*Li tann ou isit la.*_

She has some beautiful baskets. _*Li genyen kèk bèl panye.*_

Yes, you can stop there. _*Wi, ou (nou) kapab rete la.*_

I want the peanut butter. _*Mwen vle manba a.*_

They do three lessons well. _*Yo fè twa leson byen.*_

Choose the word that best describes the picture and write its letter next to the picture.

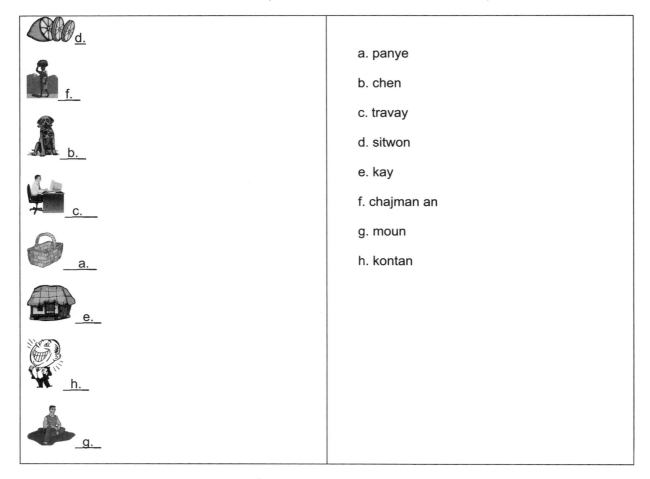

d.

f.

b.

c.

a.

e.

h.

g.

a. panye

b. chen

c. travay

d. sitwon

e. kay

f. chajman an

g. moun

h. kontan

Li kontan.

Mwen genyen yon chen.

Ou travay byen.

Lesson Four
The

Begin this lesson by reviewing the sounds of the vowels and consonants from the first three lessons. It cannot be stressed enough, how much the review of the sounds will help you prepare for each new lesson. Soon, the sounds will become routine and pronouncing a new word in Creole will become just as easy as if you were looking at a new English word. Using the flash cards, practice saying each sound. Next, review the vocabulary from lessons one through four and make flash cards for those words to add to the others.

Some tips for understanding the placement and form of the article *the*:

The rule for which form of "the" to use applies to the spelling of the word preceding the article. Review the 4 rules as stated in the Katriyèm Leson of *Creole Made Easy*.

The article **the** follows a noun phrase, and therefore the form (spelling of) used can change to fit the phrase. (A noun phrase is a group of words that takes the place of a single noun). For example:

The basket translates to **panye a**

The woman's basket as **panye fanm nan an** because "the woman's basket" is considered one word or a noun phrase.

Panye a becomes **panye.....an** because **the** takes the form that follows **nan**. In other words, **a** becomes **an** following **nan**.

The form of the article forces a pronunciation pause between the article and the word preceding it.

Using the plural **yo**:

When the subject is plural the plurality of the object is assumed. This avoids the double use of the **yo** plural indicator.

The peoples' hats – **Chapo moun yo**   *The children's toys* – **Jwèt timoun yo**
The peoples' horses – **Chwal moun yo** *The ladies' baskets* – **Panye fanm yo**
(Expressing possession is explained in the next lesson.)

Note however, that if a plural group possess only one object **the** is expressed separately and at the end of the noun phrase:

The peoples' hat – **Chapo moun yo a**   *The children's toy* – **Jwèt timoun yo a**
The peoples' horse – **Chwal moun yo a** *The ladies' basket* – **Panye fanm yo a**

In the above cases, **yo** refers to the people, children, and ladies and **a** is the singular form of **the** to specify that there is only one hat, toy, horse and basket.

In most cases, when plurality can be assumed (a person has one head, but two feet) neither the singular article, **la, a, nan**, or the plural article **yo** is used.

Tèt mwen fè mal -*My head hurts.* **Pye mwen fatige** - *My feet are tired.*
But, *Your child is sick* translates to **Pitit ou a malad**, since *pitit* can mean *child* or *children*, plurality is not known or assumed. Likewise, *Your children are sick* translates to **Pitit ou yo malad**.

Bonus Vocabulary:

devan – in front of	**dèyè** – behind	**a kote** – next to	**ant** - between

After completing the exercises, do the worksheet for this lesson.

Homework: Learn Lesson Five vocabulary. Make flash cards and add them to you vocabulary flash cards.

Worksheet Lesson Four

Using vocabulary from lesson four, fill in the correct word:

Write the Creole word in the blank:

when	_____	child	_____
over	_____	tool	_____
to come	_____	bad	_____
woman	_____	enough	_____
today	_____	where	_____

Fill in the correct singular form of *the* based on the rules explained in this lesson and then using the dictionary in the book, translate the word into English:

liv	*la*	*the book*
lapli	_____	_____
twou	_____	_____
non	_____	_____
timoun	_____	_____
zoranj	_____	_____
fanm	_____	_____
magazen	_____	_____
zouti	_____	_____
jou	_____	_____
manchèt	_____	_____
travayè	_____	_____
plim	_____	_____
repons	_____	_____
jaden	_____	_____
gonm	_____	_____
zaboka	_____	_____
sik	_____	_____
lèkol	_____	_____
ze	_____	_____
kizin	_____	_____

Using the following words write in the best word to explain the relationship:

anlè, anwo, anba, dèyè, devan, sou, nan, kole ak

the girl to the boys Ex: dèyè	the globe to the table	the pony to the horse
the professor to the blackboard	the books to the apple	the boy to the books
the man to the sink	the man to the ground	the mail to the box
the picture to the lamp	the women to each other	the rocks to the wheelbarrel

Key Lesson Four Worksheet

Using vocabulary from lesson four, fill in the correct word:

zoranj	*machin*	*chwal*	*nonm*

Write the Creole word in the blank:

when	*ki lè* or *lè*	child	*timoun* or *pitit*
over	*anlè*	tool	*zouti*
to come	*vini*	bad	*move*
woman	*fanm*	enough	*ase*
today	*jodi a*	where	*ki kote*

Fill in the correct singular form of *the* based on the rules explained in this lesson and then using the dictionary in the book, translate the word into English:

liv	*la*	*the book*
lapli	*a*	*the rain*
twou	*a*	*the hole*
non	*an*	*the name*
timoun	*nan*	*the child*
zoranj	*la*	*the orange*
fanm	*nan*	*the woman*
magazen	*an*	*the store*
zouti	*a*	*the tool*
jou	*a*	*the day*
manchèt	*la*	*the machete*
travayè	*a*	*the worker*
plim	*nan*	*the pen*
repons	*la*	*the answer*
jaden	*an*	*the garden*
gonm	*nan*	*the eraser*
zaboka	*a*	*the avacado*
sik	*la*	*the sugar*
lèkol	*la*	*the school*
ze	*a*	*the egg*
kizin	*nan*	*the kitchen*

the girl to the boysEx: *dèyè*	the globe to the table - *sou*	the pony to the horse - *devan*
the professor to the blackboard - *devan*	the books to the apple - *anba*	the books to the boy - *dèyè*
the man to the sink - *anba*	the man to the ground - *anwo*	the mail to the box - *nan*
the picture to the lamp - *anlè*	women to each other – *a kote*	the rocks to the wheelbarrel - *nan*

Lesson Five

To Express Possession

Begin this lesson by reviewing the sound flash cards. Next review the vocabulary words for lessons 1 through 5.

1. Using the possessive in Creole is really quite simple. The simplest way is to put the pronoun (the possessor) after the noun, as in the following:

my house - **kay mwen**	*our dog* – **chen nou**
John's soap – **savon Jan**	*his tool* – **zouti li**
her lime – **sitwon li**	*your orange* – **zoranj ou** (or if plural, **zoranj nou**)

Remember in lesson four the rule that to avoid the double use of **yo** when discussing possession and plurality, the plurality of the object is assumed - *the peoples' horses* – **chwal moun yo** – but if the men had only one horse, the article is expressed separately from the possessive pronoun – *the peoples' horse* – **chwal moun yo a**.

When the pronoun being used contains the **yo** form, plurality is assumed and not expressed by adding a second **yo**.
EX:
the people's dogs – **chen moun yo**

When the pronoun is not **yo**, then **yo** is used to express the plural.
EX:
your oranges – **zoranj ou yo**
our dogs – **chen nou yo**

When the pronoun is plural but possesion is singular the article is expressed separately.
EX:
the women's basket – **panye medam yo a**
Note the use of the word **medam** (*ladies*) for women. While **fanm yo** is grammatically correct, the use of the word *ladies* or **medam** is preferred.

2. The second way one can express possession is by adding the word **pa** before the pronoun. If you are confused as to which way to express ownership, you can always use the first method and be understood. However, you will hear the following and if you understand when this form is used, you will find yourself using this method just as easily.

Use **pa** before the pronoun when:
a. You are indicating ownership and you want, for effect, to emphasize or distinguish the ownership.
b. Using mine, yours, his, hers, ours, and theirs.
c. If also (or too) is used or implied.

Example a.
My dog is prettier than your dog.. - **Chen pa m' pi bèl pase chen pa w'**.
The sentence emphasizes something about mine over yours.

The large basket is his and the small basket is yours.
Gwo panye a se pa l' e ti panye a se pa w'.
The sentence distinguishes ownership between the baskets.

Example b.
It is theirs. - **Se pa yo**. (*It is* is expressed as **se** – see lesson six)
Your house is bigger than mine. - **Kay ou pi gran pase pa m'**.

Example c.
I like your house. Thank you, I like yours (your house), also.(or *Thank you, I like your house.*) – **Mwen renmen kay ou**. **Mèsi, mwen renmen (kay) pa ou, tou.**

3. The third way for expressing possession is to say **pou**, meaning *for* and is used the same as in English.
It is for him. - **Se pou li**.
The horse is for John. – **Chwal la se pou Jan.**

All three methods of expressing possession are contained in the following conversation:

We have six oranges, three for me and three for you. Mine are not large. Yours are large. Put my oranges here.

Nou genyen sis zoranj, twa pou mwen e twa pou ou. Pa m' yo pa gwo. Pa w' yo gwo. Mete zoranj mwen yo isit la.

Proceed to the worksheet for this lesson.

Learn the vocabulary for Lesson Six, making and adding the flash cards to the ones you already know. Review all vocabulary.

Worksheet Lesson Five

Write the Creole word in the blank.

begin	_____	Wednesday	_____
injure	_____	twenty	_____
Thursday	_____	church	_____
store	_____	their dog	_____
my house	_____	man	_____
Sunday	_____	buy	_____

Fill in the blank:

1. Mwen vle achte sitwon _____ yo.
I want to buy her limes.

2. _____ _____ bèl.
My house is beautiful.

3. _____ pa _____ _____.
Mine are not for you.

4. _____ pa _____.
Mine are not yours.

5. Magazen _____ genyen zouti a.
His store has the tool.

6. Mwen tann chwal _____.
I wait for your (singular) horse.

Contract:

pa mwen _____

pa ou _____

pa li _____

Translate:

His house _____

Their dog _____

His dogs_____

My big horse _____

Your (singular) basket _____

It is for her, it is not for him. _____

Conversation

Read the conversation aloud and write the translation below:

Claudette: "Mwen genyen panye ou a."
Marie: "Panye ou a piti."
Claudette: "Wi, pa m' piti. Mwen mete zoranj mwen yo nan panye ou a. Pa w' gwo."
Marie: "Oke. Pran panye mwen an. Mwen pa bezwen li."

_____

_____

_____

_____

_____

_____

_____

_____

_____

Translate:

Their houses

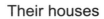

Their horse

_____

Your (plural) baskets

_____

Key Lesson Five Worksheet

Write the Creole word in the blank"

begin	*kòmanse*	Wednesday	*mèkredi*
injure	*blese*	twenty	*ven*
Thursday	*jedi*	church	*legliz*
store	*magazen*	their dog	*chen yo a*
my house	*kay mwen*	man	*nonm*
Sunday	*dimanch*	buy	*achte*

Fill in the blank:

1. Mwen vle achte sitwon *li* yo.
I want to buy her limes.

2. *Kay mwen* bèl.
My house is beautiful.

3. *Pa m'* pa *pou ou*.
Mine are not for you.

4. *Pa m'* pa *pa w'*.
Mine are not yours.

5. Magazen *li* genyen zouti a.
His store has the tool.

6. Mwen tann chwal *ou*.
I wait for your (singular) horse.

Contract:
pa mwen ___*pa m'*___
pa ou ___*pa w'*___
pa li ___*pa l'*___

Translate:
His house - *kay li*
Their dog - *chen yo a*
His dogs - *chen li yo*
My big horse - *gwo chwal mwen* or *gwo chwal pa mwen* or *gwo chwal pa m'*
Your (singular) basket - *panye ou* or *panye pa ou* or *panye pa w'*
It is for her, it is not for him. - *Li pou li, li pa pou li.*

Conversation
Claudette: "I have your basket."
Marie: "Your basket is small."
Claudette: "Yes, mine is small. I put my oranges in your basket. Yours is big."
Marie: "OK. Take my basket. I do not need it."

Their houses	Their horse	Your (plural) baskets
Kay yo	*Chwal yo a*	*Panye nou yo*

Lesson Six
Tense

In the Creole language, the verb form does not change to agree with the subject or tense. Tenses are expressed by a word before the verb. This makes expressing tenses very easy.

Past tense: The indicator word is **te**.
I go. **Mwen ale.** *I went.* **Mwen te ale.**
The subject **mwen** and the verb **ale** remain the same. Adding the word *te* before the verb is all it takes to express past tense.

Future: The future has two possible words, **pral** or **va**. In most cases, to know which to use, determine if the verb is active (action occurs) for **pral**, or if it is passive (state of being) for **va**.
Here are examples of each to help you determine which to use. If in doubt **va** is always understood and often used wtih any verb.

Note that **pral ale** – *will go* is shortened to **prale**.

Examples with **pral**:
She will do it tomorrow. **Li pral fè li demen.**
We will go there. **Nou prale la**.
The boy will finish the lesson tomorrow. **Gason an pral fini leson an demen**.

Examples with **va**:
When the road is finished it will be very good. **Lè wout la fini, li va trè bon**.
They will be tired. **Yo va fatige**.
The dogs will be tied with a rope. **Chen yo va mare ak yon kòd**.

It needs to be noted that it is common practice to omit the tense indicator if the tense can be assumed by the context of the conversation. Note the following example:
Yè, mwen pa t' kontan avèk ou paske ou vini ta – *Yestersay, I was not happy with you because you came late.* Literally the sentence says *because you come late*, but it is assumed since it was yesterday or in the past that *I was not happy*, the act of coming is also in the past. It is never incorrect to include the tense indicator.

Continuous/ongoing: The word **ap** is inserted before the verb.

He is working well. **Li ap travay byen.**
You are speaking loudly. **Ou ap pale fò.**
They are giving him the tools. **Yo ap bay li zouti yo.**

Negative: **Pa** is inserted before the verb to express a negative and comes before the tense indicator.

Li kapab vini (*He can come.*) becomes **Li pa kapab vini**. (*He cannot come.*)

Li te vini (*He came*) becomes **Li pa te vini**, usually contracted to **Li pa t' vini** (*He did not come.*)

When expressing **pa ap**, **pa pral** or **pa va**, the contracted form **pa'p** is used.

He is not coming. **Li pa ap vini** becomes **Li pa'p vini.**

He will not come. **Li pa pral vini** becomes **Li pa'p vini.**

He won't come. **Li pa va vini** becomes **Li pa'p vini.**

The only way to distinguish between the above sentences is in the context of the conversation.

Do the worksheets for Lesson Six and learn the vocabulary for Lesson Seven.

Worksheet Lesson Six

Change the sentence to indicate past tense.

Yo ale legliz.

_____

Medam yo genyen bèl zoranj.

_____

Li travay.

_____

Nou vini ak chwal nou yo.

_____

Correct the following sentences.

Li ale yè.

_____

Yo fè li demen.

_____

Rewrite the following sentences, putting them in the negative.

Gason an vini jodi a.

_____

Frè li va vini jedi.

_____

Mwen ap pale.

_____

Change the tense indicators to their contracted forms:

Yo pa ap vini. _____

Pastè a pa te pale yè _____

Claire pa pral vini demen _____

Wout la pa va bon _____

Doktè a pa pral ba ou li _____

Li pa te fini _____

Choose from the words below and write the correct vocabulary word under the picture:

doktè, mesye, bra, pwofesè, pastè, elèv, lapli, pye bwa

Key Worksheet Lesson Six

Change the sentence to indicate past tense.

Yo ale legliz.
Yo te ale legliz.

Medam yo genyen bèl zoranj.
Medam yo te genyen bèl zoranj.

Li travay.
Li te travay.

Nou vini ak chwal nou yo.
Nou te vini ak chwal nou yo.

Correct the following sentences.

Li ale yè.
Li te ale yè.

Yo fè li demen.
Yo pral fè li demen.

Rewrite the following sentences, putting them in the negative.

Gason an vini jodi a.
Gason an pa vini jodi a.

Frè li va vini jedi.
Frè li pa' p vini jedi.

Mwen ap pale.
Mwen pa' p pale.

Change the tense indicators to their contracted forms:

Yo pa ap vini. *Yo pa'p vini.*
Pastè a pa te pale yè. *Pastè a pa t' pale yè.*
Claire pa pral vini demen. *Claire pa'p vini demen.*
Wout la pa va bon. *Wout la pa'p bon.*
Doktè a pa pral ba ou li. *Doktè a pa'p ba ou li.*
Li pa te fini. *Li pa t' fini.*

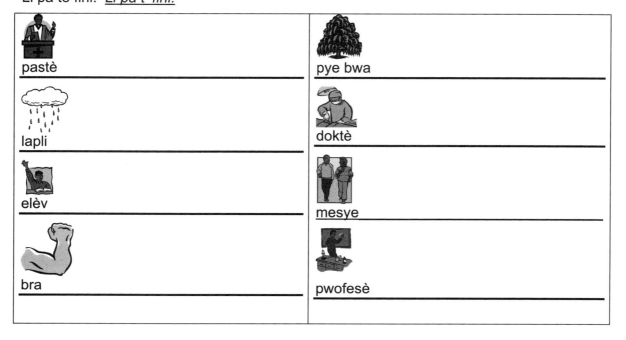

pastè	pye bwa
lapli	doktè
elèv	mesye
bra	pwofesè

Lesson Seven
The Verb "To Be"

You should have the vocabulary for lesson seven memorized before beginning this worksheet. Review all your vocabulary learned by using the flash cards.

You have been making simple sentences using a subject, verb and sometimes an object. In most cases the verb *to be* (is, am, are, etc.) is not used. There are cases, however, where the verb is used. In these cases, the verb *to be* is translated as **se**.

If a sentence is equating a noun with the subject, **se** comes after the subject and before the noun. Ex: *I am a doctor* becomes **Mwen se doktè**. *He is a pastor* becomes **Li se pastè**. **Se** in these cases means *am* or *is*. Think of this as a balance or scale. If what is on one side of the scale is equal to what is on the other side, **se** is used.

Pierre *is* a teacher.	Pierre **se** pwofesè.
Jean Claude *is* a doctor.	Jean Claude **se** doktè.
I *am* a student	Mwen **se** elèv.
She *is* a merchant.	Li **se** machann
The computer *is* a tool.	Odinatè a **se** yon zouti.

Note in all of the above examples, the subject is being equated to the object.

When the subject is being described or when the subject does not equal the object, **se** is not used.

Pierre is not a teacher.	Pierre **pa** pwofesè.
Pierre was a teacher.	Pierre **te** pwofesè
The merchant is there.	Machann nan la.
I am not a student.	Mwen **pa** elèv.
The computer is broken.	Odinatè a kase.

Note that in the above, the subject is either being described or is not equal to the object.

Another way to understand this is to look at the relationship of the subject with what is being expressed. A general rule could be stated that if the sentence is in a *noun/adjective* format, the verb *to be* is not expressed. In other words, do not use **se**. If the subject is in a *noun/noun format*, but not in the negative, the verb *to be* is expressed. In other words, use **se**.

Se is also used to express *it is*. Ex: *It is easy* becomes **Se fasil**. In this case, **li** (it) is replaced by **se**. A general rule to know when to use **li** and when to use **se** follows:

Li is used more when referring to a person or object (something physical or tangible). In other words, something you can see. A task, time, or concept is more often expressed by **se**. A sentence about a house would use **li** while the general area aournd the house would be **se**.

The key to the above rules for expressing *it is*, is to remember that if the subject is something *tangible (something you can hold or see)*, and *is not equating itself to the object*, do not use **se**.

It was is expressed by adding the past tense indicator **te** after **se**. *It was a good thing* becomes **Se te yon bon bagay**. The same rules apply to the subject and object and tangible or concept as stated above.

It was big. Li **te** gwo. (This is referring to an object being described – noun/adjective format.)

It was a good idea. **Se te** yon bon lide. (This is referring to a concept or something intangible. One cannot hold or touch an idea.)

The other form of expressing is, am or are is expressed by using **ye** and is usually used when forming a question and comes at the end of the question. Ex: *Where are the horses?* translates to **Ki kote chwal yo ye?**

Bonus vocabulary:

sweater	**chanday**
next	**pwochen**
wish (hope)	**swete**
week	**semenn**
perhaps	**pètèt**
month	**mwa**
problem	**pwoblèm**
chance	**chans**
than, that	**ke**
let's	**an nou, an n'**
true	**vre**
enter	**antre**

Do the worksheets for Lesson Seven and learn the vocabulary for Lesson Eight.

Worksheet Lesson Seven

Of the following sentences mark the ones that express the "to be" as "se"

_____She is very pretty.

_____You are a teacher

_____The house is small.

_____I am a good worker.

_____It is big.

_____Where are you going?

_____It is a good thing to do.

_____The children are happy.

_____He went home.

_____It was hard.

_____The car is red.

_____Where is the paper?

_____He is a student.

_____He is studying.

Translate:

It was not easy. _____

I am lazy. _____

Who are you? _____

Where are the people? _____

The child is finished with his work. _____

My arm is injured. _____

Where are you going? _____

The man is working. _____

It is useful. _____

It is true._____

The worker is going out. _____

Yours is mine. Mine is yours _____

Converstaion:

Read the conversation aloud and then translate it below.

"Ki sa w'ap fè?"
"M'ap fè yon chanday."
"Pou ki moun li ye?"
"Li pou manman mwen."
"Mwen pa kapab fè yon chanday."
"Se fasil pou mwen. Mwen va fini li demen. Manman mwen ap vini semenn pwochen."
"Li va kontan ke ou fè yon chanday pou li."
"Mwen swete sa se vre."

_____

_____

_____

_____

_____

_____

_____

_____

_____

_____

_____

_____

_____

Key Worksheet Lesson Seven

Of the following sentences mark the ones that use the "to be" form "se"

_____She is very pretty.
__X__You are a teacher
_____The house is small.
__X__I am a good worker.
_____It is big.
_____Where are you going?
__X__It is a good thing to do.
_____The children are happy.
_____He went home.
__X__It was hard.
_____The car is red.
_____Where is the paper?
__X__He is a student.
_____He is studying.

Translate:
It was not easy. *Li pa te fasil*
I am lazy. *Mwen parese.*
Who are you? *Ki moun ou ye?*
Where are the people? *Ki kote moun yo ye?*
The child is finished with his work. *Timoun nan fini ak travay li.*
My arm is injured. *Bra mwen blese.*
Where are you going? *Ki kote ou prale?*
The man is working. *Nonm nan ap travay.*
It is useful. *Se itil.*
It is true. *Se vre.*
The worker is going out. *Travayè a ap soti.*
Yours is mine. Mine is yours. - *Pa w' se pa m'. Pa m' se pa w'.*

"Ki sa w'ap fè?"
"M'ap fè yon chanday."
"Pou ki moun li ye?"
"Li pou manman mwen."
"Mwen pa kapab fè yon chanday."
"Se fasil pou mwen. Mwen va fini li demen. Manman mwen ap vini semenn pwochen."
"Li va kontan ke ou fè yon chanday pou li."
"Mwen swete sa se vre."

"What are you doing?"
"I am making a sweater."
"Who is it for?"
"It is for my mother."
"I cannot make a sweater."
"It is easy for me. I will finish it tomorrow. My mother is coming next week."
"She will be happy that you made a sweater for her."
"I hope that is true."

Lesson Eight
Contractions

You should have the vocabulary for lesson eight memorized before beginning this worksheet. Review all your vocabulary learned by using the flash cards.

Contractions are used extensively in the Creole language but are not necessary for speaking the language. <u>When in doubt you can always form your sentences without contractions and be understood.</u> However, because others use contractions, it will be easier for you to understand what they are saying if you know the more common contractions.

Pa te (the negative past) is contracted as **pa t'**.
Ex: **Li pa te fini travay li yè** becomes **Li pa t' fini travay li yè**.

Pral or **va** (the future) is contracted as **a**.
Ex: **Li pral fini travay li demen** becomes **L'a fini travay li demen**.

When using **ap** (continuous action) the pronoun preceding **ap** is contracted.
Ex: **Li ap fini travay li** becomes **L'ap fini travay li**.

The pronoun **mwen** is the only one that is contracted at the beginning of a sentence unless the word following the pronoun begins with a vowel. So while you would say **M' vle** for *Mwen vle*, you would not say L' vle or Y' vle. Note the following examples:

I want to come - **Mwen vle vini** - **M' vle vini**
He wants to come – **Li vle vini**.
They want to come – **Yo vle vini**

I do it if I want – **M' fè l' si m' vle**
He does it if he wants – **Li fè l' si l' vle**
They do it if they want – **Yo fè l' si yo vle**

Note the difference in the following examples when the word following the pronouns starts with a vowel.

I buy it – **Mwen achte li** – **M'achte li** – **M'achte l'**
She buys it – **Li achte li** – **L'achte li** - **L'achte l'**
You buy it – **Ou achte li** – **W'achte li** – **W'achte l'**
We (You –plural) buy it – **Nou achte li** – **N'achte li** – **N'achte l'**
They buy it – **Yo achte li** – **Y'achte li** – **Y'achte l'**

In the future tense all pronouns may be contracted:

I will come if I want – **Mwen pral vini si mwen vle - M'a vini si m' vle**

You will come if you want – **Ou pral vini si ou vle – W'a vini si ou vle**. (the second ou is not contracted because w' vle is not easily pronounced.)

He will come if he wants – **Li pral vini si li vle - L' a vini si l' vle**.

We (You – plural) will come if we want – **Nou pral vini si nou vle – N'a vini si n' vle**

They will come if they want – **Yo pral vini so yo vle – Y'a vini si yo vle**. (the second yo is not contracted because y' vle is not easily pronounced.)

Because **nou** means both the plural *you* and *we, us* or *ours*, while not a specific grammatical rule, there is a tendency (but not a rule) in speech to use **nou** to mean you and the contracted **n'** to me us. The above example might be translated as such:

We will come if we want – **Nou pral vini si nou vle – N'a vini si n' vle**

You will come if you want – **Nou pral vini si nou vle**

Review the contractions as explained in Lesson Eight.

Do the worksheets for Lesson Eight and learn the vocabulary for Lesson Nine.

Worksheet Lesson Eight

Underline the words that can be contracted in the following sentences:

1. Kay pa mwen gwo.
2. Yo pral vini demen.
3. Mwen vle wè kay pa li.
4. Nou achte li nan gwo magazen an.
5. Li pa ap ale lekòl jodi a men li va ale demen.
6. Mwen kapab fè li.
7. Yo va vini tan-zan-tan.
8. Nou va bati kay pa ou ansanm.
9. Li te vle dis zoranj men mwen pa te genyen dis.
10. Yo pa te kapab rale li.

Rewrite the above sentences using the contracted words where possible:

1. _____
2. _____
3. _____
4. _____
5. _____
6. _____
7. _____
8. _____
9. _____
10. _____

Translate the above sentences into English:

1. _____
2. _____
3. _____
4. _____
5. _____
6. _____
7. _____
8. _____
9. _____
10. _____

Translation:

Read the following paragraph aloud and then translate it below (Use the dictionary in *Creole Made Easy*, if necessary.):

Tann mwen. M'ap vini. M' vle ale avèk ou. Si m' pa ale kounye a, m' pa'p ka ale. M' vle achte kèk panye pou ze mwen yo. Li pral pi fasil pou vann ze mwen yo si m' mete yo nan panye yo. Ou pral achte panye tou. N'a achte yo ansanm. Claire ap vini avèk nou. Li pa vle achte panye, men l'a achte sitwon pou manman l'.

_____

_____

_____

_____

_____

_____

_____

_____

_____

_____

_____

Choose the correct sentence:

_____

a. Paulette ap soti lakay li.   b. Paulette ap antre lakay li.

Key Worksheet Lesson Eight

Underline the words that can be contracted in the following sentences:
   11. Kay <u>pa mwen</u> gwo.
   12. <u>Yo pral</u> vini demen.
   13. <u>Mwen vle</u> wè kay <u>pa li</u>.
   14. <u>Nou achte li</u> nan gwo magazen an.
   15. Li<u> pa ap</u> ale lekòl jodi a men <u>li va</u> ale demen.
   16. <u>Mwen kapab fè li</u>.
   17. <u>Yo va</u> vini tan-zan-tan.
   18. <u>Nou va</u> bati kay <u>pa ou</u> ansanm.
   19. Li te vle dis zoranj men <u>mwen pa te</u> genyen dis.
   20. Yo <u>pa te</u> <u>kapab</u> <u>rale li</u>.

Rewrite the above sentences using the contracted words where possible:
1. *Kay pa m' gwo.*
2. *Y'a vini demen.*
3. *M' vle wè kay pa l'.*
4. *N' achte l' nan gwo magazen an.*
5. *Li p'ap ale lekòl jodi a men l'a ale demen.*
6. *M' ka fè l'.*
7. *Y'a vini tan-zan-tan.*
8. *N'a bati kay pa w' ansanm.*
9. *Li te vle dis zoranj men m' pa t' genyen dis.*
10. *Yo pa t' ka rale l'.*

Translate the above sentences into English:
1. My house is big.
2. They will come tomorrow.
3. I want to go to your house.
4. We buy it in a big store.
5. He did not go to school today, but he will go tomorrow.
6. I can do it. (I can make it.)
7. They will come from time to time.
8. We will build your house together.
9. She (He) wanted ten oranges but I did not have ten.
10. They could not pull it.

 Tann mwen. M'ap vini. M' vle ale avèk ou. Si m' pa ale kounye a, m' pa'p ka ale. M' vle achte kèk panye pou ze mwen yo. Li pral* pi fasil pou vann ze mwen yo si m' mete yo nan panye yo. Ou pral achte panye tou. N'a achte yo ansanm. Claire ap vini avèk nou. Li pa vle achte panye, men l'a achte sitwon pou manman l'.

   Wait for me. I am coming. I want to go with you. If I don't go now, I will not be able to go. I want to buy some baskets for my eggs. It will be easier to sell my eggs if I put them in the baskets. You will buy baskets, too. We will buy them together. Claire is coming with us. She does not want to buy baskets, but she will buy limes for her mother.

*L'ap pi fasil could also be used as the context of the conversation indicates future.

_____ *b.*

a. Paulette ap soti lakay li.   b. Paulette ap antre lakay li.

Lesson Nine
There is, there are

Genyen or **gen** (the abbreviated form of **genyen**) is used when expressing *there is* or *there are*. Literally it means *to have* or *to get*.

There are oranges in the basket translates to:
Gen zoranj nan panye a.
Literally: *Have oranges in the basket* or *Got oranges in the basket*.

Note that you do not translate oranges to zoranj yo because **gen** and **genyen** default to the plural. If you wanted to say *the oranges are in the basket* you would say: *Zoranj yo nan panye a.* But when using *there is* and *there are*, the article is omitted unless you want to specify that there is only one orange in the basket. Then you would say:
Gen yon zoranj nan panye a or *there is an orange in the basket.*

Past tense:
To say *there were* add the past tense indicator **te** in front of **gen**.
There were oranges in the basket translates to:
Te gen zoranj nan panye a.

Future tense:
To say *there will be* add the future tense indicator **pral** in front of **gen**.
There will be oranges in the basket translates to:
Pral gen zoranj nan panye a.

Note the word *there* (place) in Vocabulary Nine is translated as **la** or **la a**. **La** is used to refer to a general direction or area while **la a** is a specific place or spot. Sometimes **bò la a** (over there) is also used to refer to a general place or direction.

Mete bwat la bò la a or **Mete bwat la la**   - *Put the box over there.*

Mete bwat la la a – *Put the box there.* (right there)

In the second example you are giving instructions to put the box in a specific spot.

Do the worksheets for Lesson Nine and learn the vocabulary for Lesson Ten.

Worksheet Lesson Nine

Write the translation below the sentence:

There are too many pens.

_____

Gen yon pwoblèm (problem) ak machin ou.

_____

Te gen twòp raje nan ranje a.

_____

There are two today.

_____

Tomorrow there will be six.

_____

Remember there are pens in the desk.

_____

Pral gen zouti pou fè travay la.

_____

Gen kawoutchou dèyè kay la

_____

Translation:

Read the following paragraph aloud and then translate it below:

Gen moun k'ap vini demen pou bati yon kay. Yo va bezwen bon zouti. Pètèt yo ka achte zouti pa w'. Yo mande nou jwen travayè ki ka travay ak yo. Yo pa konenn ki lè y'a fini. Yo swete fini nan twa mwa. Sa se bon pou travayè yo paske y'a genyen bon travay pou twa mwa. Pètèt y'a fini anvan twa mwa. N'a wè.

Key Worksheet Lesson Nine

Write the translation below the sentence:

There are too many pens.
Gen twòp plim

Gen yon pwoblèm ak machin ou.
There is a problem with your car.

Te gen twòp raje nan ranje a.
There were too many weeds in the row.

There are two today.
Gen de jodi a.

Tomorrow there will be six.
Demen pral gen sis.

Remember there are pens in the desk.
Sonje gen plim nan biwo a.

Pral gen zouti pou fè travay la.
There will be tools to do the work.

Gen kawoutchou dèyè kay la.
There are tires behind the house.

Read the following paragraph aloud and then translate it below:

Gen moun k'ap vini demen pou bati yon kay. Yo va bezwen bon zouti. Pètèt yo ka achte zouti pa w'. Yo mande nou jwen travayè ki ka travay ak yo. Yo pa konenn ki lè y'a fini. Yo swete fini nan twa mwa. Sa se bon pou travayè yo paske y'a genyen bon travay pou twa mwa. Pètèt y'a fini anvan twa mwa. N'a wè.

There are people who are coming tomorrow to build a house. They will need good tools. Perhaps they can buy your tools. They asked us to find workers who can work with them. They do not know when they will finish. They hope to finish in three months. This is good for the workers because they will have good work for three months. Perhaps, they will finish before three months. We will see.

Lesson Ten
Asking Questions

There are two kinds of questions in Creole; identification and information.

Identification questions:

In Creole, a question seeking to identify something begins with **ki** and is followed by the subject (that which needs identifying). The *is* in this case is translated as **sa ye** or **ye** at the end of the question.

Ex:

What book is this? – **Ki liv sa ye?** (Literally – What book this is?)

Who is this? – **Ki moun sa ye?** (Literally – What person this is?)

Who are you? – **Ki moun ou ye?** (Literally – What person you are?)

If the noun is not known it can be replaced with **sa**.

What book is this? – **Ki liv sa ye?**

What is this? – **Ki sa sa ye?**

Information questions:

In Creole, questions of information begin with **ki** and are followed with the subject (about which information is needed). **Ye** is used at the end of the sentence to express *is*, using the same rules as explained in Lesson Seven.

What time will you come? – **Ki lè w'a vini?**

Who will cook the food? – **Ki moun ki pral kwit manje a?**

How (What way) are you called? – **Ki jan ou rele?**

What color is your hat? – **Ki koulè chapo ou ye?**

Which is it? – **Kilès li ye?**

Which hat is yours? – **Kilès chapo ki pou ou?** (literally: which hat is for you?)

Where do you go...? – **Ki kote ou ale...?**

Where are you? – **Ki kote ou ye?**

Who is there? **Ki moun ki la?**

Which desk is better for you? **Kilès biwo ki pi bon pou ou?**

Note in the above the **ki** follows the *noun*, so the sentence becomes **kilès** *noun* **ki**.

Note that there are several ways to ask someone his/her name.
The most common is the example above – **Ki jan ou rele?**

What is your name is literally translated as **Ki sa non ou ye?** But this is never said. Instead **Ki non ou?** is used (*What name you?*).

It is also correct and common to say **Kouman ou rele?** or literally, *How you called?*

Do the worksheets for Lesson Ten and learn the vocabulary for Lesson Eleven.

Worksheet for Lesson Ten

Matching:
Write the correct letter in the space provided.

_____Where are you?   a. Ki lè l'a vini?

_____How are you?   b. Pouki sa li kite li?

_____Who is doing it?   c. Kilès ki pi gwo?

_____Why did he leave it?   d. Ki kote ou ye?

_____When will she come?   e. Kouman ou ye?

_____Are you going to your house?   f. Ki moun k'ap vini demen?

_____Where did you put it?   g. Ki lè w'a fè li?

_____Which one do you want?   h. Kilès ou vle?

_____Which is bigger?   i. Ki moun k'ap fè li?

_____Who is coming tomorrow?   j. Eske ou prale lakay ou?

_____Why is she not working?   k. Ki kote ou te mete li?

_____When will you do it?   l. Pouki sa li p'ap travay?

 Translate:

Ki sa w'ap kwit?

_____

Make a question out of the following statements, translating them into Creole. Use the word in the parenthesis to guide you.

He is coming. (Is)_____

_____

She will go. (Why)_____

_____

The man has the papers. (Does)_____

_____

Your name is Pierre. (Is)_____

_____

The book is here. (Where)_____

_____

You are doing that. (What)_____

_____

The computer works very fast. (Why)_____

_____

They remember where it is. (Do)_____

_____

Her dog's name is ... (What is)_____

_____

Jean lives here. (Where)_____

_____

You will go. (Where)_____

_____

He did this. (Why)_____

_____

Key Worksheet Lesson Ten

Matching:

Write correct letter in the space provided.

<u>d.</u> Where are you?

<u>e.</u> How are you?

<u>i.</u> Who is doing it?

<u>b.</u> Why did he leave it?

<u>a.</u> When will she come?

<u>j.</u> Are you going to your house?

<u>k.</u> Where did you put it?

<u>h.</u> Which one do you want?

<u>c.</u> Which is bigger?

<u>f.</u> Who is coming tomorrow?

<u>l.</u> Why is she not working?

<u>g.</u> When will you do it?

a. Ki lè l'a vini?

b. Pouki sa li kite li?

c. Kilès ki pi gwo?

d. Ki kote ou ye?

e. Kouman ou ye?

f. Ki moun k'ap vini demen?

g. Ki lè w'a fè li?

h. Kilès ou vle?

i. Ki moun k'ap fè li?

j. Eske ou prale lakay ou?

k. Ki kote ou te mete li?

l. Pouki sa li p'ap travay?

 Translate: Ki sa w'ap kwit? *What are you cooking?*

Make a question out of the following statements, translating them into Creole. Use the word in the parenthesis to guide you.

He is coming. (Is) *Eske l'ap vini?*

She will go. (Why) *Pouki sa li prale?*

The man has the papers. (Does) *Eske nonm nan genyen papye yo?*

Your name is Pierre. (Is) *Eske ou rele Pierre?* or *Eske non ou se Pierre?(not commonly used, but grammatically correct)*

The book is here. (Where) *Ki kote liv la ye?*

You are doing that. (What) *Ki sa w'ap fè?*

The computer works very fast. (Why) *Pouki sa òdinatè a travay trè vit?* or *Pouki sa òdinatè a travay vit anpil?*

They remember where it is. (Do) *Eske yo sonje ki kote li ye?*

Her dog's name is (What is) *Kouman chen li a rele?* or *Ki jan chen li a rele?* or *Ki non chen li a?*

Jean lives here. (Where) *Ki kote Jan rete?*

You will go. (Where) *Ki kote ou prale?*

He did this. (Why) *Pouki sa li te fè sa?*

Lesson Eleven
Comparison

Let's review the words used when making comparisons:

pi - the "*er*" of the English language, used with an adjective to express older, bigger, better, etc.
Ex:
Kay li te bati a pi bon – *The house he built is better*

pase – expresses *than* after an adjective (bigger than, taller than, etc.) and is never used alone but always used with **pi**.– **pi** *adj* **pase**
Ex:
Kay li te bati a pi bon pase kay Jan – *The house he built is better than Jean's house.*

pase tout – the "*est*" of the English language, used with an adjective to express *biggest, oldest*, etc. and is never used alone, but always used with **pi**. (**pi** *adj.* **pase tout**. This is only used when there is a special reason to emphasize the idea of *best of all*. The above form - **pi** *adj* **pase** - is usually preferred.
Ex:
Kay li te bati a pi bon pase tout. – *The house he built is the best of all.*

To further emphasize *best of all*, **pase yo tout** can be used. **Li pi gran pase tout** (*He is the oldest*) could also be said **Li pi gran pase yo tout**, meaning *he is the oldest of everyone*.

Li panse li pi bon pase yo tout. - *She thinks she is better than all of them.*

plis – is used to express *more*, or *more than*

Ex:
Li genyen plis zoranj – *She has more oranges*
Li genyen plis ke mwen - *She has more than I*

It is important to understand that there is often more than one way to phrase a sentence. Take the example sentence - *The prettiest mangoes will sell before the others.*
There are three ways this could be said in Creole.
Pi bèl mango yo pral vann anvan lezòt yo.
Mango ki pi bèl yo pral vann anvan lezòt yo.
Se mango ki pi bèl yo ki pral vann anvan lezòt yo.

While all three ways are grammatically correct and would be understood, the third example is preferred. This literally translated means "*It is the prettiest mangoes which will sell before the others.*" This is not normally said in English as mangoes is plural and English does not say "It are the prettiest mangoes."

This is a good time to go over the use of **bon** and **byen**. As in English there is a distinction between the words *good* and *well*. Something can be good while an act or action can be done well.
Ex:
The mango is good – **Mango an bon**
You do that well – **Ou fè sa byen**

It is good when you work well – **Li bon lè ou travay byen**.
Note that in this sentence, **li** is used with **bon**. **Bon** is used with an object or person, as only an object or person can be good.

In Creole, the pharse - **Se byen sa** – *(It is well)* is used to respond to good news concerning a situation. **Se** is used with **byen** as opposed to **li**.

good – **bon**
well – **byen**
It is good – **Li bon**
It is well – **Se byen**

Se ki refers to a fairly specific noun. If it is used with a general noun it is used in such a way as to separate the noun in some way from others.
Ex:
It is the vendor who comes early who sells more – **Se machann ki vini bonè ki vann plis**. (this specific vendor as opposed to the other vendors)

Do the worksheets for Lesson Eleven and learn the vocabulary for Lesson Twelve.

Worksheet for Lesson Eleven

Using "pi gwo" and "pi piti" label the pictures below.

Translate the sentences below:

He types better than Violet.

_____

You have more than I.

_____

It rained more today than yesterday. (note – *to rain* is **fè lapli**)

_____

Elizabeth writes the best of all.

_____

Pierre is older than you.

_____

(Interesting fact: In rural Haiti, the main meal of the day is cooked midday in an open pot over a fire of wood or charcoal.)

Conversation:

Read the conversation aloud and then translate below:

"Manje a te pi bon jodi a pase yè."

"Wi, se vre."

"Eske ou konnen pouki sa?"

"Manje jodi a te genyen plis sèl."

"Oke, se sa. Zoranj yo te pi bèl tou."

"Manje jodi a pi bon pase tout."

_____

_____

_____

_____

_____

_____

_____

_____

_____

_____

Key Worksheets Lesson Eleven

Using "pi gwo" and "pi piti" label the pictures below.

pi gwo	pi piti
pi piti	pi gwo

pi piti	pi gwo
pi gwo	pi piti

Translate the sentences below:

He types better than Violet.
Li tape pi byen pase Violet.

You have more than I.
Ou genyen plis pase mwen. or *Ou genyen plis pase m'.*

It rained more today than yesterday. (Note – *to rain* is "make rain" - *fè lapli*)
Li fè plis lapli jodi a pase yè,

Elizabeth writes the best of all.
Elizabeth ekri pi byen pase tout.

Pierre is older than you.
Pierre pi gran pase ou or *Pierre pi gran pase w'.*

 Conversation:

"The food was better today than yesterday."
"Yes, that's true."
"Do you know why?"
"Today's food had more salt".
"OK, that's it. The oranges were better, too.
"Today's food was the best."

Lesson Twelve
Too, too much, less, very, so, so that

Too or *also* – **tou**
Ex: **Mwen vle ale tou** – *I want to go, too*

Too much – **twòp**
Ex: **Ou ban nou twòp** – *You give us too much*

Note however that if **twòp** comes before an adjective the endng "p" is omitted making the word **twò**. Another way to understand this is that if **twòp** is being used to mean *too* (as in *too big* or *too little,* not meaning *also*) as opposed to *too much*, the ending "p" is dropped.
Ex: **Li te vini twò ta** – *He came too late*

Less - **mwens**
Ex: **Pa ban nou mwens ke yè** – *Don't give us less than yesterday*

Note however that if **mwens** comes before an adjective the endng "s" is omitted making the word **mwen**. Or in other words if **mwens** is being used to mean *less* as in *not as* the ending "s" is dropped.
Ex: **Bagay yo mwen chè nan magazen sa a** – *The things are less (not as) expensive in this store.* Do not confuse **mwen** as in *me* or *I*, with **mwen** as in *less*. **Bagay mwen yo mwen chè** – *My things are less expensive*

Very – **trè, anpil**
Ex: **Mwen trè kontan** – *I am very happy*

Note however if **anpil** is used for very, it implies extremely happy with, **anpil** emphasizing *happy*. Remember that **anpil** comes after the adjective.
Ex: **Mwen kontan anpil** – *I am very happy*.

So much/many – **si tèlman**
Ex: **Li pale si tèlman dousman** – *She speaks so slowly.*

So much/many that - **si tèlman ___ ke**
Ex: **Li te kondwi si tèlman dousman ke nou rive an reta** – *She drove so slowly that we arrived late.*

So that, in order to – **pou**
Ex: **Mwen prale pou ou kapab rete** – *I will go so that you can stay.*

When referring to age in children use **piti** and **gran** for *young* and *old* as opposed to **jenn** and **vye**. **Li pi piti** – *He is younger* and **Li pi gran** – *He is older.*

It is grammatically correct to say **vye** for an adult, but it is avoided because **vye** also means *old, worn out* or *worthless*. For an adult use **laj** (age).
Ou genyen plis laj pase mwen – *You are older than I (literally – You have more age than I.)*

Do the worksheets for Lesson Twelve and learn the vocabulary for Lesson Thirteen.

Worksheet Lesson Twelve

Translate:

She is so much older than you.

_____

Your child is too old.

_____

Your child is older than all the others.

_____

This food has too much salt.

_____

We speak so slowly.

_____

The food is very good.

_____

It was well made. (prepared)

_____

The food is so good that I am eating too much.

_____

You speak Creole well.

_____

You speak Creole so well.

_____

This is a good thing.

_____

It is good when you work well.

_____

I make fewer (less) mistakes now than before.

_____

I want to come too.

_____

Celine has 6 children, three of them young, three of them old.

_____

Your child is not so old.

_____

Puzzle Fun

Down:
2. heavy
3. very
4. wait
6. work
8. since
12. early
13. come
14. horse
15. leave

Across
1. unfortunately
5. all
7. during, while
9. write
10. to show ongoing action
11. fast
12. give
15. can
16. only
17. useful

Key Worksheet Lesson Twelve

She is so much older than you.
Li si tèlman pi gran pase ou.

Your child is too old.
Pitit ou a twò gran.

Your child is older than all the others.
Pitit ou a pi gran pase tout lòt yo.

This food has too much salt.
Manje sa a genyen twòp sèl.

We speak so slowly.
Nou pale si tèlman dousman.

The food is very good.
Manje a trè bon. or *Manje a bon anpil.*

It was well made. (prepared)
Li te byen pare.

The food is so good that I am eating too much.
Manje a si tèlman bon ke m'ap manje twòp.

You speak Creole well.
Ou pale Kreyòl byen.

You speak Creole so well.
Ou pale Kreyòl si tèlman byen.

This is a good thing.
Sa se yon bon bagay.

It is good when you work well.
Li bon lè ou travay byen.

I make less mistakes now than before.
Mwen fè mwens fot kounye a pase anvan.

I want to come too.
Mwen vle vini, tou. (M' vle vini, tou.)

Celine has 6 children, three of them young, three of them old.
Celine genyen sis pitit, twa nan yo piti, twa nan yo gran.

Your child is not so old.
Pitit ou a pa si tèlman gran.

Puzzle Fun:

Lesson Thirteen
The Conditional – would, could, should, might, etc.

Using the conditional tense in Creole is not difficult. As with the other tense forms, the verb remains the same and becomes conditional with the adding of a word before the verb.

Would and *would have* are both expressed with **ta**. In the other conditional forms **ta** is changed to **te** to indicate past tense.

could -**ta ka** becomes **te ka**
should - **ta dwe** becomes **te dwe**

Ex:
Would - **ta**
He would come – **Li ta vini**
He would have come – **Li ta vini**

Could – **ta ka**
He could come – **Li ta ka vini.**
He could have come – **Li te ka vini**

May – **ta ka**
He may come – **Li ta ka vini**
He might have come – **Li te ka vini**

Should – **ta dwe**
He should come – **Li ta dwe vini**
He should have come – **Li te dwe vini**

Ought – **ta dwe**
He ought to come – **Li ta dwe vini**
He ought to have come – **Li te dwe vini**

The negative form of the conditional adds **pa** before **ta**.

Ex:
He ought not to go out late – **Li pa ta dwe soti ta**
I should not like him to do that – **Mwen pa ta renmen li fè sa**
Jean could not come if he did not have a car – **Jan pa ta ka vini si li pa t' genyen yon machin** (**pa t'** is the contracted form of **pa te**)

Note that when *may* is used as *can (might be able or might do)*, it is translated as **ta kapab** or **ta ka** as above, but when *may* is being used to give permission, it is translated as **mèt**.

Ex:
Mwen ta ka rete ta – *I may (might) stay late*
Ou mèt rete ta – *You may stay late.*

Do the worksheets for Lesson Thirteen and learn the vocabulary for Lesson Fourteen.

Worksheet Lesson Thirteen

Translation

Read the paragraph aloud and translate below. (Use the *Creole Made Easy* dictionary if necessary.)

Moun yo pral pi kontan avèk travay ou si ou rive a lè. Ou dwe kite lakay ou pi bonè pou ou pa rive twò ta. Ou se pitit mwen. Sa pa fè mwen kontan lè ou pa fè sa ou dwe fè. Tanpri, pitit mwen, pa fè mwen wont devan moun sa yo. Yo bay ou travay pou ede ou. Yo pa oblije kenbe ou nan travay la si ou pa travay byen. Pa di yo ou ta vini a lè si ou pa t' gen pwoblèm. Yo pa ta dwe tande eskiz ou. Mwen ta kontan pou ou pa fè sa ankò.

_____

_____

_____

_____

_____

_____

_____

_____

_____

_____

Using the hint at the end of the sentence, correct the following sentences, then translate:

Li travay byen si bra li pa te fè mal. (would)

_____

_____

Jules fè li si li te ka vini. (would)

_____

_____

Mwen ka fini ak travay mwen si mwen te ka rete. (could)

_____

_____

Nou dwe fini sa nou di nou ta fè. (should)

_____

_____

Word Jumble

Translate the English word into Creole and find it in the word jumble. Words go across and down, but not diagonally or up.

He, late, three, say, tie, again, ten, you, not, tight fit, more, beat, tie, arm, empty, pour, want, child, where, money, head, go, untie, corner, boat

M	B	D	I	S	E	A	L
K	W	E	N	S	E	N	I
V	C	M	O	U	N	K	W
T	W	A	T	N	K	Ò	B
L	B	R	A	R	O	U	A
V	L	E	L	P	T	È	T
I	D	V	E	O	E	K	O
D	B	J	P	I	T	I	T
E	R	M	A	N	M	A	N

Key Worksheet Lesson Thirteen

Translation

Moun yo pral pi kontan avèk travay ou si ou rive a lè. Ou dwe kite lakay ou pi bonè pou ou pa rive twò ta. Ou se pitit mwen. Sa pa fè mwen kontan lè ou pa fè sa ou dwe fè. Tanpri, pitit mwen, pa fè mwen wont devan moun sa yo. Yo bay ou travay pou ede ou. Yo pa oblije kenbe ou nan travay la si ou pa travay byen. Pa di yo ou ta vini a lè si ou pa t' gen pwoblèm. Yo pa ta dwe tande eskiz ou. Mwen ta kontan pou ou pa fè sa ankò.

The people will be happier with your work if you arrive on time. You ought to leave your house earlier so that you do not arrive too late. You are my child. It does not make me happy when you do not do what you ought to do. Please, my child, do not make me ashamed in front of these people. They give you work to help you. They are not obligated to keep you in the work if you do not work well. Do not tell them you would come on time if you did not have problems. They should not hear your excuse. I would be happy for you to not do this again.

Using the hint at the end of the sentence, correct the following sentences:
Li travay byen si bra li pa te fè mal. (would)
Li ta travay byen si bra li pa te fè mal.
He would work well if his arm did not hurt.

Jules fè li si li te ka vini. (would)
Jules ta fè li si li te ka vini.
Jules would do it if he could come.

Mwen ka fini ak travay mwen si mwen ta ka rete. (could)
Mwen ta ka fini ak travay mwen si mwen te ka rete.
I would finish with my work if I could stay.

Nou dwe fini sa nou di nou ta fè. (should)
Nou ta dwe fini sa nou di nou ta fè.
We should finish what we said we would do.

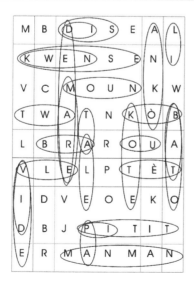

Lesson Fourteen
The Passive

In most cases, the Creole language avoids using the passive voice. To translate a sentence from the passive voice in English (subject is acted upon by the verb) into Creole simply turn it around into the active voice (the subject performs the action).
Passive voice: *The book is being read by the class.*
Active voice: *The class is reading the book.*
To Say:
The house was painted turn the sentence around to *They painted the house.* **Yo te pentire kay la.**
The soup was already eaten by the children becomes *The children already ate the soup* or **Timoun yo te deja manje soup la**.

One common exception to the active/passive rule includes the passive forms of *to do (done)* and *to make (made)* which are either expressed as **fèt,** used in the passive or **fè**, used in the active voice.

The work was well done - **Travay la te byen fèt**
They did the work well – **Yo te fè travay la byen**
The dress was well made – **Wòb la te byen fèt**
She made the dress well – **Li te fè wòb la byen**

When an action was taken by someone but it cannot be attributed to any specific person, **yo** (*they*) is used as the subject when the sentence is turned into the Creole active voice.

We have been told that already - **Yo te di nou sa deja.** (*They told us that already.*)
They were given - **Yo te ba yo.** (*They gave them*)
The vegetables were delivered early today – **Yo te livre legim yo bonè jodi a.**
(Note that one uses the impersonal **yo** even if only one person delivered the vegetable because it is not known who it was.)

Do the worksheets for Lesson Fourteen and learn the vocabulary for Lesson Fifteen.

Bonus Vocabulary

dodin	fotèy	chosèt
òlòj	almanak	abitasyon

Worksheet Lesson Fourteen

Change the following sentences from the passive voice to the active voice and translate into Creole (use the *Creole Made Easy* dictionary if necessary):

The rocking chair was broken by the child.

_____

The sewing is being done by the women.

_____

Your horse was ridden by Claude.

_____

The bed was already made.

_____

The paper was written with a computer by Vernicia.

_____

The preaching was done by the pastor.

_____

The toys were given to the children.

_____

Men were given work by the boss.

_____

The food was spoiled by rain.

_____

The car was fixed by Paul.

_____

The flag was raised late this morning.

_____

Write the correct letter of the translation next to the Creole sentence:

_____Mwen genyen yon chen.   a. Tell the men to come tomorrow.

_____Pye bwa yo piti.   b. The trees are small.

_____Di mesye yo vini demen.   c. They will go to the store on Saturday.

_____Li dwe vizite manman li.   d. I have a dog.

_____Yo prale nan magazen an samdi.   e. I will give them my horse.

_____M'a ba yo chwal pa m'.   f. She ought to visit her mother.

Vocabulary:

Write the correct word beneath the picture (use the *Creole Made Easy* dictionary if necessary):

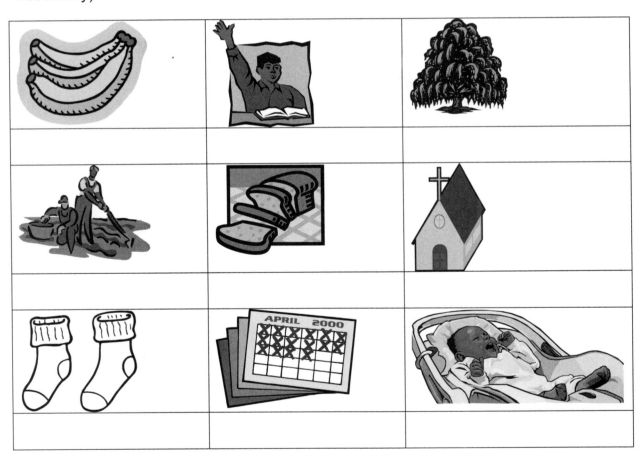

Key Worksheet Lesson Fourteen

The rocking chair was broken by the child.
Timoun nan te kase dodin nan.

The sewing is being done by the women.
Medam yo (Fanm yo) ap fè kouti a.

Your horse was ridden by Claude.
Claude te monte chwal ou.

The bed was already made.
Kabann nan te deja fèt.

The story was written with a computer by Vernicia.
Vernicia te ekri istwa a avèk yon òdinatè.

The preaching was done by the pastor.
Se pastè a ki te preche.

The toys were given to the children.
Yo te bay timoun yo jwèt yo.

Men were given work by the boss.
Bòs la te bay mesye yo travay.

The food was spoiled by rain.
Lapli te gate manje a.

The car was fixed by Paul.
Paul te ranje machin nan.

The flag was raised late this morning.
Yo te monte drapo a ta maten an.

Write the correct letter of the translation next to the Creole sentence:

<u>d.</u> Mwen genyen yon chen.   a. Tell the men to come tomorrow.
<u>b.</u> Pye bwa yo piti.   b. The trees are small.
<u>a.</u> Di mesye yo vini demen.   c. They will go to the store on Saturday.
<u>f.</u> Li dwe vizite manman li.   d. I have a dog.
<u>c.</u> Yo prale nan magazen an samdi.   e. I will give them my horse.
<u>e.</u> M'a ba yo chwal pa m'.   f. She ought to visit her mother.

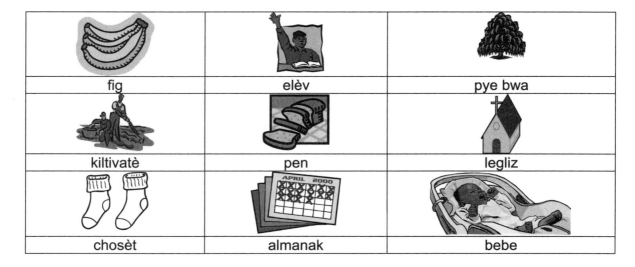

fig	elèv	pye bwa
kiltivatè	pen	legliz
chosèt	almanak	bebe

Lesson Fifteen
This, that, these, those

In Creole, the demonstrative determiners *this, that, these* and *those* are expressed differently depending on whether they are being used as adjectives or as pronouns.

The adjective forms (demonstrative adjective) of *this, that, these* and *those* are used with nouns to modify and identify nouns or noun phrases. The adjective form is used with a subject or noun to specify which one(s). *This house needs to be painted.* **Kay sa a bezwen pentire.**

Unlike in English, the Creole adjective follows the noun when used with *this*, *that these* and *those*. *This house* becomes **kay sa a**.

As adjectives:	This – **sa a**	These – **sa yo**
	That – **sila a (sa a)**	Those – **sila yo (sa yo)**

Those limes were not good, these limes are good – **Sitwon sila yo pa te bon, sitwon sa yo bon**.
That house needs to be repaired – **Kay sila a bezwen repare.**
Those dogs are mean but this dog is nice. **Chen sila yo mechan men chen sa a janti.**

(Note: As with the proper use of *me* and *I* in English, there is frequent confusion between **sila a** and **sa a** and between **sila yo** an **sa yo** in Creole. Increasingly, **sila a** and **sila yo** are being replaced by **sa a** and **sa yo** in common speech.)

The pronoun forms (demonstrative pronouns) of *this, that, these,* and *those* (sa, sa, sa yo, sa yo) replace nouns or pronouns. *This should be done.* **Sa dwe fèt.**

As pronouns:	This – **sa**	These – **sa yo**
	That – **sa**	Those – **sa yo**

When used as subjects the pronoun forms can be used to refer either to objects or to persons.

This is my father – **Sa se papa mwen**.
That is my book – **Sa se liv mwen**.
This is a pretty hat – **Sa se yon bèl chapo**

Note that **se** is used between the pronoun and object. This follows the rule presented in Lesson Seven. The verb *to be* translates as **se** before a noun or pronoun that means the same thing as the subject. *This, that, these* and *those* when used as the subject refer to the noun following, specific or implied.

Do the worksheets for Lesson Fifteen.

Worksheet Lesson Fifteen

Find the error in the Creole sentence and fix it.

That house is small.
Kay sila yo piti.

_____

Those cats do not like these dogs.
Chat sila yo pa renmen chen sa a.

_____

That computer is faster than this computer.
Odinatè sa yo pi vit pase òdinatè sa a.

_____

I like this pen better than that one.
Mwen pito plim sa a pase sa yo.

_____

This rice is very good.
Diri sa yo bon anpil.

_____

This is the child who was sick.
Sila yo se timoun nan ki te malad.

_____

These are the rocks we prefer.
Sa se pwa nou pito yo.

_____

Those books are heavy.
Liv sa yo lou.

_____

That is a good horse.
Sila a se yon bon chwal.

_____

Those are the good limes.
Sa se bon sitwon yo.

_____

Write the correct sentence under the picture:

Fanm nan ap vann zoranj Fanm nan ap kwit yon gato Fanm nan ap fè cheve li	Mesye a ap repare machin li Mesye a ap koupe pye bwa Mesye a ap travay nan jaden li
_____	_____
Anne ap koud yon rido Anne ap kwit yon patat Anne ap fèmen vit la	Ti moun nan ap bay chat yo manje Ti moun nan ap monte chwal la Ti moun nan ap bay zwazo yo manje
_____	_____
Philippe ap dòmi nan kabann li Philippe ap ekri yon lèt Philippe ap pale nan telefòn	Pwofesè a ap ekri ak lakrè Pwofesè a ap ranje chèz yo Pwofese a pa'p travay jodi a
_____	_____

Key Worksheet Lesson Fifteen

That house is small.
Kay sila yo piti.
Kay sila a piti.

Those cats do not like these dogs.
Chat sila yo pa renmen chen sa a.
Chat sila yo pa renmen chen sa yo.

That computer is faster than this computer.
Odinatè sa yo pi vit pase òdinatè sa a.
Odinatè sila a pi vit pase òdinatè sa a.

I like this pen better than that one.
Mwen pito plim sa a pase sa yo.
Mwen pito plim sa a pase sila a.

This rice is very good.
Diri sa yo bon anpil.
Diri sa a bon anpil.

This is the child who was sick.
Sila yo se timoun nan ki te malad.
Sa se timoun nan ki te malad.

These are the rocks we prefer.
Sa se pwa nou pito yo.
Sa yo se wòch nou pito yo.

Those books are heavy.
Liv sa yo lou.
Liv sila yo lou.

That is a good horse.
Sila a se yon bon chwal.
Sa se yon bon chwal.

Those are the good limes.
Sa se bon sitwon.
Sa yo se bon sitwon

Write the correct sentence under the picture:

Fanm nan ap kwit yon gato.	*Mesye a ap travay nan jaden li*
Anne ap koud yon rido	*Ti moun nan ap bay zwazo yo manje*
Philippe ap pale nan telefòn	*Pwofesè a ap ekri ak lakrè*

Lesson Sixteen
Some, some of

The Creole word **kèk** means *some* and is always plural. *Some of* is translated as **kèk nan** (and is also always plural).

The professor reads some books – **Pwofesè a li kèk liv.**
The professor reads some of his books – **Pwofesè a li kèk nan liv li yo.**

In the cases when *some* comes before a singular noun and a word indicating a part or piece of the noun is needed, **kèk** is not used. Words indicating a part of a whole like **yon ti**, **yon moso** or **yon pati** are used for some and **yon moso nan** and **yon pati nan** are used for *some of*.

I need some cloth to finish this dress. **Mwen bezwen yon mòso twal pou fini wòb la.**

Please give me some of the rice. **Tanpri ban m' yon pati nan diri a.**

I want some water to drink. **Mwen vle yon ti dlo pou bwè.**
Note that **yon ti** (a little) is used with water as you cannot have a piece or part of water.

Some is expressed with **de** (**gen de**) when referring to a general group rather than a specific person.

Some workers never work well – **Gen de travayè ki pa janm travay byen.**
Some children never finish their food – **Gen de timoun ki pa janm fini manje yo.**

Following the worksheet for Lesson Sixteen there is a review worksheet covering Lessons 1-16.

KONPLIMAN! CONGRATULATIONS! You have finished all sixteen lessons and are well on your way to speaking Creole. Review any lessons you are not sure about and continue to learn new vocabulary words. You are now equipped with the tools you need to **pale kreyòl!** Practice speaking by using the examples throughout the text with different nouns and verbs from the dictionary at the back of the textbook.

Worksheet Lesson Sixteen

Correct the following sentences:

1. Mwen bezwen kèk pen pou m' fè sandwich mwen.

_____

2. Nou ta dwe voye yon pati liv pou elèv yo.

_____

3. Kèk moun pa janm rive a lè.

_____

4. Jules vle achte kèk nan flè pou madanm li.

_____

5. Tanpri, ban nou yon mòso dlo.

_____

6. Machann nan vann mwen kèk ze li yo.

_____

Translate the corrected sentences:

1. _____

_____

2. _____

_____

3. _____

_____

4. _____

_____

5. _____

_____

6. _____

_____

Match the two sentences that best go together
(If necessary, use the dictionary in the back of *Creole Made Easy*):

_____	Jean se elèv	a. Mwen prale legliz
_____	Li fè cho	b. Mwen bezwen voye kèk nan fig yo bay li
_____	Jodi a se dimanch	c. Ouvri fenèt la
_____	Mwen pa genyen zoranj	d. Li prale lekòl
_____	Yo pa ka vini	e. Ou pa bezwen vini demen
_____	Mwen malad anpil	f. Mwen bezwen ale nan mache a
_____	Li midi	g. Mwen pa ka vini travay jodi a
_____	Madanm nan ansent	h. Ale kay doktè avèk li
_____	Zanmi mwen renmen tout kalite fwi	i. Li tèlman fè lapli machin yo pa ka rive
_____	Ou travay tèlman vit ou deja fini travay la	j. Li pral akouche mwa pwochen
_____	Chen an te mòde timoun nan	k. Li ap manje

Just for fun translate:
He reads it.

_____

Key Worksheet Lesson Sixteen

Correct the following sentences:

1. Mwen bezwen kèk pen pou m' fè sandwich mwen.

Mwen bezwen yon moso pen pou m' fè sandwich mwen.

2. Nou ta dwe achte yon pati liv pou elèv yo.

Nou ta dwe achte kèk liv pou elèv yo.

3. Kèk moun pa janm rive a lè.

Gen de moun ki pa janm rive a lè.

4. Jules vle achte kèk nan flè pou madanm li.

Jules vle achte kèk flè pou madanm li.

5. Tanpri, ban nou yon mòso dlo.

Tanpri, ban nou yon ti dlo.

6. Machann nan vann mwen kèk ze li yo.

Machann nan vann mwen kèk nan ze li yo.

Translate the corrected sentences:
1. *I need a piece of bread to make my sandwich.*
2. *We (You) ought to buy some books for the students.*
3. *Some people never arrive on time.*
4. *Jules wants to buy some flowers for his wife.*
5. *Please give us some water to drink.*
6. *The vendor sold me some of her eggs.*

Match the two sentences that best go together
(If necessary, use the dictionary in the back of *Creole Made Easy*):

d. Jean se elèv	a. Mwen prale legliz
c. Li fè cho	b. Mwen bezwen voye kèk nan fig yo bay li
a. Jodi a se dimanch	c. Ouvri fenèt la
f. Mwen pa genyen zoranj	d. Li prale lekòl
i. Yo pa ka vini	e. Ou pa bezwen vini demen
g. Mwen malad anpil	f. Mwen bezwen ale nan mache a
k. Li midi	g. Mwen pa ka vini travay jodi a
j. Madanm nan ansent	h. Ale kay doktè avèk li
b. Zanmi mwen renmen tout kalite fwi	i. Li tèlman fè lapli machin yo pa ka rive
e. Ou travay tèlman vit ou deja fini travay la	j. Li pral akouche mwa pwochen
h. Chen an te mòde timoun nan	k. Li ap manje

He reads it.
Li li li.

Final Review Lessons 1-16

Using the clue at the end of the sentence, put the following sentences into a question:

Paula has oranges and limes. (how many)

_____

They are coming tomorrow morning before I go to work. (are)

_____

You want to buy my car. (do)

_____

She always does that. (does)

_____

Marie wants this one. (which)

_____

He is going to his house. (is)

_____

Translate the following paragraph.
Patrick has too many books. He wants to give you some. Which books do you want?
How many books can you take? I will tell him tomorrow when I see him what you want.
You should go to his house and look at the books.

_____

_____

_____

_____

_____

_____

_____

Find the mistakes in the following sentences and correct them. Then translate the sentences:

1. Travay li plis bon.

_____

2. Machin li plis nan bon pase tout.

_____

3. Se bon lè ou fè sa ou dwe fè.

_____

4. Se pwofesè a prepare ki fè pi bon leson.

_____

5. Li genyen pi timoun ke mwen

_____

Replace the quantities with some.

Five people always sleep late.

_____

I want a cup of water.

_____

We should give the students ten pens.

_____

I bought six of her eggs yesterday.

_____

I am giving you a bread.

_____

Puzzle fun:

DOWN:

1. Brase
2. Apre jodi a
3. Ou bezwen youn pou ouvri yon pòt
5. en, de, twa, ____
6. Pitit mwen genyen sis _____
7. La
10. Rakonte yon _____
12. Ou pa konnen ki ____ pou ale
14. Bwè yon tas ____

ACROSS

1. Sa ou bwè lè ou malad
4. Lè li fè nwa ou pase sa a
5. Jwèt timoun
7. Bay, ba, ____
8. Youn ou lòt
9. Bwason ki fèt ak zoranj
11 Si ou fè yon bagay anpil fwa ou gen sa
13. Chemen
15. Yon fore genyen pye ____
16. Distans ant de baygay

Read the following conversation aloud and then translate:

Mwen bezwen kèk wòch pou bati kay mwen. Eske ou konnen ki kote mwen kapab jwen yo? Si mwen kapab jwen anpil, m' pral voye kèk nan yo bay sè mwen. Mari li ap bati yon kay, tou. Nou bezwen lapli tonbe pou nou genyen yon ti dlo. Si nou pa gen dlo nou pa ka brase mòtye a.

_____

_____

_____

_____

_____

_____

_____

_____

_____

_____

Translate:

My horse _____

His horse _____

Your (singular) horse _____

Our horse _____

Our horses _____

Your (plural) horse _____

Your (plural) horses _____

Their horse _____

Their horses _____

Pick out the sentences that use se (to be) and translate them in Creole
He is a student.
Your car is new.
It is not so difficult.
It is good to do that.
They are very happy

_____

_____

_____

_____

_____

Correct the following sentence:
Ki kote chwal yo?

_____

Correct the errors below. Write the correct form of "the" in the space provided.
liv nan _____

bonbon la_____

chemen an_____

nonm la _____

jaden nan_____

fanm la_____

twou la _____

leson a _____

panye mwen nan _____

panye li a _____

Translate the following sentences:

Those dogs are bigger than these.

_____

This hat is pretty.

_____

Write the correct word under the picture with the correct form of the:

Translate:

There are some limes in the basket for you.

_____

There will be time to do that.

_____

Put the bag over there.

_____

We had more yesterday.

_____

We have less today.

_____

There are so many over there that we have no room.

_____

I will do it so you do not need to do it.

_____

There are so many limes that some of them will spoil.

_____

The work was done.

_____

The women are not ready yet.

_____

Using the hint at the end of the sentence correct the following sentences:

Mwen fè li si mwen kapab. (would)

_____

Ou ede manman ou ak travay li. (should)

_____

Nou travay si ou ta peye nou. (might)

_____

Pierre e Paul fini travay yo anvan yo te ale. (should have)

_____

Change to past tense:

Nou achte li yè.

_____

Li ban nou zouti li.

_____

Change to future tense:

Yo fatige.

_____

Manman mwen fè manje a.

_____

Change to continuous action:

Celia tann lòt yo.

_____

Change to the negative future:

Li vini dimanch.

_____

Rewrite the following sentences using contractions where possible, then translate the sentence:

Mwen vle vini wè ou lè mwen kapab jwen yon woulib.

_____

_____

Li pral fini pentire kay pa mwen demen.

_____

_____

Yo pral vini si li vle.

_____

_____

Mwen pa te ale lekòl yè.

_____

_____

Li ap manje bonbon an si ou pa di li pa manje li.

_____

_____

Zouti pa li pèdí.

_____

_____

Li pa te fini travay li.

_____

_____

Translate:

Mwen fini ak tout leson yo. Kounye a m' ka pale kreyòl.
Mwen fè trè byen.

_____

_____

_____

_____

_____

Key Final Review Lessons 1-16

Put the following sentences into a question:

Paula has oranges and limes.
Konbyen zoranj e konbyen sitwon Paula genyen?
They are coming tomorrow morning before I go to work.
Eske y'ap vini demen maten anvan mwen ale nan travay?
You want to buy my car.
Eske ou vle achte machin mwen?
She always does that.
Eske li toujou fè sa?
Marie wants this one.
Kilès Marie vle?.
He is going to his house.
Eske li prale lakay li?

Translate the following paragraph.
Patrick has too many books. He wants to give you some. Which books do you want? How many books can you take? I will tell him tomorrow when I see him what you want. You should go to his house and look at the books.

Patrick genyen twòp liv. Li vle ba ou kèk nan yo. Kilès liv ou vle? Konbyen liv ou ka pran? M'a di li demen lè mwen wè li konbyen ou vle. Ou ta dwe ale lakay li pou gade liv yo.

Find the mistakes in the following sentences and correct them. Then translate the sentences:

1. Travay li plis bon.
Travay li pi bon.
2. Machin li plis nan bon pase tout.
Machin li pi bon pase tout.
3. Se bon lè ou fè sa ou dwe fè.
Li bon lè ou fè sa ou dwe fè.
4. Se pwofesè a prepare ki bay pi bon leson.
Se pwofesè a ki prepare ki bay pi bon leson.
5. Li genyen pi timoun ke mwen
Li genyen plis timoun ke mwen.

Replace the quantities with some.
Five people always sleep late.
Gen de moun ki toujou dòmi ta.
I want a cup of water.
Mwen vle yon ti dlo.
We should give the students ten pens.
Nou dwe bay elèv yo kèk plim.
I bought six of her eggs yesterday.
Mwen te achte kèk nan ze li yo yè.
I am giving you a bread.
M'ap ba ou yon moso pen.

Puzzle fun:

	¹M	E		²D	I	³K	A	M	A	N			
	E			E		L							
	⁴L	I		M	Y	è				⁵K	⁶A	P	
	A			E				⁷B	A	N			
	N			⁸N	E	N	P	ò	T				
	⁹J	¹⁰I						L					
	¹¹E	S		P	E	R	I	A	N		¹²S		
		T						A			A		
		¹³W	O	U	¹⁴T						N		
¹⁵B	W	A				¹⁶E	S	P	A	S			

DOWN:

1. Brase

2. Apre jodi a

3. Ou bezwen youn pou ouvri yon pòt

5. en, de, twa. ____

6. Pitit mwen genyen sis _____

7. La

10. Rakonte yon _____

12. Ou pa konnen ki ____ pou ale

14. Bwè yon tas ____

ACROSS

1. Sa ou bwè lè ou malad

4. Lè li fè nwa ou pase sa a

5. Jwèt timoun

7. Bay, ba, ____

8. Youn ou lòt

9. Bwason ki fèt ak zoranj

11 Si ou fè yon bagay anpil fwa ou gen sa

13. Chemen

15. Yon fore genyen pye ____

16. Distans ant de baygay

Read the following conversation aloud and then translate:

Mwen bezwen kèk wòch pou bati kay mwen. Eske ou konnen kote mwen kapab jwen yo? Si mwen kapab jwen anpil, m' pral voye kèk nan yo bay sè mwen. Mari li ap bati yon kay, tou. Nou bezwen lapli tonbe pou nou genyen yon ti dlo. Si nou pa gen dlo nou pa ka brase mòtye a.

I need some rocks to build my house. Do you know where I can find them? If I can find many, I will send some of them to give my sister. Her husband is building a house, too. We need rain to fall so we have a little water. If we do not have water we cannot mix the mortar.

Translate:

My horse *Chwal mwen*

His horse *Chwal li*

Your (singular) horse *Chwal ou*

Our horse *Chwal nou a*

Our horses *Chwal nou yo*

Your (plural) horse *Chwal nou a*

Your (plural) horses *Chwal nou yo*

Their horse *Chwal yo a*

Their horses *Chwal yo*

Pick out the sentences that use se (to be) and translate them in Creole
He is a student. - *Li se elèv.*
It is not so difficult. *- Se pa si tèlman difisil.*

Correct the following sentence:
Ki kote chwal yo?
Ki kote chwal yo ye?

Correct the errors below. Write the correct form of the in the space provided.
liv nan *liv la*
bonbon la *bonbon an*
chemen an *chemen an*
nonm la *nonm nan*
jaden nan *jaden an*
fanm la *fanm nan*
twou la *twou a*
leson a *leson an*
panye mwen nan *panye mwen an*
panye li a *panye li a*

Translate the following sentences:
Those dogs are bigger than these.
Chen sila yo pi gwo pase sa yo.
This hat is pretty.
Chapo sa a bèl.

Write the correct word under the picture with the correct form of the:

chen an	òlòj la	kay yo	pye bwa a
pastè a	chosèt yo	fig yo	panye a
melon an (melon dlo a)	pwofesè a	zannanna a, anana a,	almanak la
pwason an	pitit fi a, timoun nan, elèv la	lekòl la	machin yo

Translate:

There are some limes in the basket for you.
Genyen (Gen) kèk sitwon nan panye a pou ou.
There will be time to do that.
Pral gen (genyen) tan pou fè sa.
Put the bag over there.
Mete sak la la or Mete sak la bò la a.
We had more yesterday.
Nou te genyen plis yè.
We have less today.
Nou genyen mwens jodi a.
There are so many over there that we have no room.
Genyen (Gen) si tèlman anpil la (bò la a) ke nou pa gen (genyen) plas.
I will do it so you do not need to do it.
M'a fè l' (li) pou ou pa bezwen fè l' (li).
There are so many limes that some of them will spoil.
Genyen (Gen) si tèlman sitwon ke kèk nan yo pral gate.
The work was done.
Travay la te fèt.
The women are not ready yet.
Medam yo (Fanm yo) poko pare.

Using the hint at the end of the sentence rewrite the following sentences:
Mwen fè li si mwen kapab. (would)
Mwen ta fè li si mwen ta kapab.
Ou ede manman ou ak travay li. (should)
Ou ta dwe ede manman ou ak travay li.
Nou travay si ou ta peye nou. (might)
Nou ta ka travay si ou ta peye nou.
Pierre e Paul fini travay yo anvan yo te ale. (should have)
Pierre e Paul te dwe fini travay yo anvan yo te ale.

Change to past tense:
Nou achte li yè.
Nou te achte li yè.
Li ban nou zouti li.
Li te ban nou zouti li.

Change to future tense:
Yo fatige.
Yo pral fatige.
Manman mwen fè manje a.
Manman mwen pral fè manje a.

Change to continuous action:
Celia tann lòt yo.
Celia ap tann lòt yo.

Change to the negative future:
Li vini dimanch.
Li pa'p vini dimanch.

Rewrite the following sentences using contractions where possible, then translate the sentence:
Mwen vle vini wè ou lè mwen kapab jwen yon woulib.
M' vle vini wè ou lè m' ka jwen yon woulib.
I want to come see you when I can find a ride.

Li pral fini pentire kay pa mwen demen.
L'a fini pentire kay pa m' demen.
He will finish painting my house tomorrow.

Yo pral vini si li vle.
Y'a vini si l' vle.
They will come if she (he) wants.

Mwen pa te ale lekòl yè.
M' pa't ale lekòl yè.
I did not go to school yesterday.

Li ap manje bonbon an si ou pa di li pa manje li.
L'ap manje bonbon an si ou pa di l' pa manje l'.
He will eat the cookie if you don't tell him not to eat it.

Zouti pa li yo pèdí.
Zouti pa l' yo pèdi.
His tools are lost.

Li pa te fini travay li.
Li pa t' fini travay li.
He didn't finish his work.

Translate:

Mwen fini ak tout leson yo. Kounye a m' ka pale kreyòl.
Mwen fè trè byen.

I am finished with all the lessons. Now I can speak Creole. I did very well.

Supplemental Section

If you have sucessfully competed the sixteen lessons of Creole Made Easy, you are speaking Creole. To further aid you in the process of understanding and communicating, the following seven chapters have been designed as a practical, applied Creole guide for non-speaking Creole residents and visitors of Haiti. These chapters are relevant and useful to both the "short term" and more permanent resident.

They are organized into the following topics:

    Numbers and Time
    Months, Days, Seasons and Weather
    Colors
    Family and Friends
    Marketplace and Food
    Around the House
    Health and Medicine

Numbers and Time

one – one hundred:

en	one	**senkanteyen**	fifty one
de	two	**senkannde**	fifty two
twa	three	**senkanntwa**	fifty three
kat	four	**senkannkat**	fifty four
senk	five	**senkannsenk**	fifty five
sis	six	**senkannsis**	fifty six
sèt	seven	**senkannsèt**	fifty seven
uit	eight	**senkantuit**	fifty eight
nèf	nine	**senkantnèf**	fifty nine
dis	ten	**swasant**	sixty
onz	eleven	**swasanteyen**	sixty one
douz	twelve	**swasannde**	sixty two
trèz	thirteen	**swasanntwa**	sixty three
katòz	fourteen	**swasannkat**	sixty four
kenz	fifteen	**swasannsenk**	sixty five
sèz	sixteen	**swasannsis**	sixty six
disèt	seventeen	**swasannsèt**	sixty seven
dizuit	eighteen	**swasantuit**	sixty eight
diznèf	nineteen	**swasantnèf**	sixty nine
ven	twenty	**swasanndis**	seventy
venteyen	twenty one	**swasanteonz**	seventy one
vennde	twenty two	**swasanndouz**	seventy two
venntwa	twenty three	**swasanntrèz**	seventy three
vennkat	twenty four	**swasannkatòz**	seventy four
vennsenk	twenty five	**swasannkenz**	seventy five
vennsis	twenty six	**swasannsèz**	seventy six
vennsèt	twenty seven	**swasanndisèt**	seventy seven
ventuit	twenty eight	**swasanndizuit**	seventy eight
ventnèf	twenty nine	**swasanndisnèf**	seventy nine
trant	thirty	**katreven**	eighty
tranteyen	thirty one	**katrevenen**	eighty one
trannde	thirty two	**katrevende**	eighty two
tranntwa	thirty three	**katreventwa**	eighty three
trannkat	thirty four	**katrevenkat**	eighty four
trannsenk	thirty five	**katrevensenk**	eighty five
trannsis	thirty six	**katrevensis**	eighty six
trannsèt	thirty seven	**katrevensèt**	eighty seven
trantuit	thirty eight	**katrevenuit**	eighty eight
trantnèf	thirty nine	**katrevennèf**	eighty nine
karant	forty	**katrevendis**	ninety
karanteyen	forty one	**katrevenonz**	ninety one
karannde	forty two	**katrevendouz**	ninety two
karanntwa	forty three	**katreventrèz**	ninety three
karannkat	forty four	**katrevenkatòz**	ninety four
karannsenk	forty five	**katrevenkenz**	ninety five
karannsis	forty six	**katrevensèz**	ninety six
karannsèt	forty seven	**katrevendisèt**	ninety seven
karantuit	forty eight	**katrevendizuit**	ninety eight
karantnèf	forty nine	**katrevendisnèf**	ninety nine
senkant	fifty	**san**	one hundred

It needs to be noted that the *number one* is either **en** or **youn**, depending on how it is used. **En** is the name of the *number one*, but **youn** is always used for saying the *quantiy of one. How many horses are in the picture? One* - **Youn**

Note: As explained in Lesson One, the number *eight* and its derivatives are the only words in Creole that begin with the letter *u*. Remember that **uit** is pronouned by saying the words *you eat* very quickly.

Counting by Tens:

10	dis
20	ven
30	trant
40	karant
50	senkant
60	swasant
70	swasanndis
80	katreven
90	katrevendis
100	san

To count into the *hundreds*, start with one hundred and add the remaining number to it.

101 - **san en**	102 - **san de**
122 - **san vennde**	185 - **san katrevensenk**

Two hundred is expressed the same as **de san** or *two hundred*.

200 – de san	300 – twa san	400 – kat san	500 – senk san
600 – sis san	700 – sèt san	800 – uit san	900 – nèf san

One thousand is **mil**. To continue counting into the *thousands* do exactly the same as for hundreds. *One thousand one hundred* (1100) is **mil san**, *one thousand two hundred* (1200) is **mil de san**, *four thousand three hundred forty six* (4,346) **kat mil twa san karantsis**, etc.

A *million* is **yon milyon**. *Two million* is **de milyon**, and so forth.

EX:
12 – **douz**
112 – **san douz**
1,112 – **mil san douz**
11,112 – **onz mil san douz**
111,112 – **san onz mil san douz**
1,111,112 – **yon milyon san onz mil san douz**

Telling Time

Vocabulary for telling time:

clock – **revèy**	four o'clock – **katrè**
large clock (grandfather clock) – **pandil**	five o'clock – **senkè**
watch – **mont**	six o'clock – **sizè**
hour - **è**	seven o'clock – **sètè**
half hour – **edmi**	eight o'clock – **uitè**
quarter till – **mwenka**	nine o'clock – **nevè**
quarter past - **eka**	ten o'clock – **dizè**
one o'clock – **inè**	eleven o'clock – **onzè**
two o'clock – **dezè**	noon – **midi**
three o'clock – **twazè**	midnight – **minwi**

Half past can also be said by adding **trant** to the hour. In other words, 1:30 can be said **inè edmi** (*one and a half hour*) or **inè trant** (*one thirty*). While **inè trant** is correct, **inè edmi** is the more common usage.

In the same way, fifteen or a quarter past the hour can be said by adding **kenz** (fifteen) to the hour. 5:15 – **senkè eka** (five and a quarter hour) or **senkè kenz** (five fifteen).

In Creole, twelve o'clock (douzè) is never used. It is always *noon* or *midnight* to distinguish if it is day or night. To say 12:05 if it is five minutes past noon, say **midi senk** or "*noon five.*" To say 12:05 if it is five minutes past midnight, say **minwi senk** or "*midnight five.*"

Anything other than quarter past, half past, or quarter till is the hour with the number of minutes either after the hour or before the next hour. If the time is 30 minutes or less after the hour, it is expressed by saying the hour with the number of minutes.

3:16	4:18	9:22	7:12
twazè sèz	**katrè dizuit**	**nevè vennde**	**sètè douz**

If the time is more the thirty minutes past the hour, it is traditionally expressed by saying the next hour minus the number of minutes needed to reach the next hour. In other words, 7:44 is not expressed as sètè karantkat. It is expressed as uitè mwen sèz.

3:52	4: 34	9:40
katrè mwen uit	**senkè mwen vennsis**	**dizè mwen ven**

Remember that the *s* is dropped in **mwens** (*less*) when used before adjectives. This is also true when using **mwens** (**mwen**) in telling time.

Note: With the increasing use of digital clocks and watches, it is becoming more common to only say the hour with the number of minutes.

EX:

dizè senkannkat

There are two ways to ask what time an event or action will or did occur.

Ki lè – *what time or when* – a general time period
A ki lè – *at what time* – a more specific time or hour

When did the worker come? **Ki lè travayè a te vini?** *He came today.* - **Li te vini jodi a.**

At what time did the worker come? - **A ki lè travayè a vini?** *He came at 8:30.* - **Li te vini a uitè edmi.**

Worksheet Numbers and Time

Write the correct number beneath the picture:

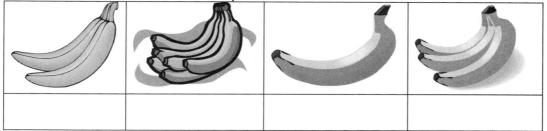

What time is it? Write the time below the clock or fill in the hands to match the time.

		twazè mwen ven	
	senkè mwen dis		
	midi	sètè senk	
	uitè mwen senk		dizè

Match and write the correct letter answer below the time

2:10	Midnight	6:15	7:45	11:07

5:27	4:35	8:12	10:38	9:08

a. uitè douz   b. uitè mwen kenz   c. nevè uit   d. minwi   e. senkè vennsèt
f. dezè dis   g. senkè mwen vennsenk   h. sizè eka   i. onzè sèt j. onzè mwen
                                                                      vennde

Follow the example and write the correct answer to the math problems in the space provided:

3 +2	10 +40	7 +2	6 +1	12 +10
senk				
11 +30	5 +5	15 +15	100 +100	25 +12

Fill in the blanks with the correct number word:

en, de, twa, _____, senk, sis, _____, uit, _____, dis, _____,

_____, trèz, _____,kenz, _____, disèt, dizuit, _____, ven,

_____, vennde, venntwa, _____, vennsenk

How many do you see? Write the correct Creole number word.

Key Worksheet Numbers and Time

Write the correct number beneath the picture:

de	*sis*	*en (youn)*	*twa*

What time is it? Write the time below the clock or fill in the hands to match the time.

twazè	*inè trant or inè edmi*	*twazè mwen ven*	*onzè ven*
sizè	*senkè mwen dis*	*katrè*	*uitè*
nevè	*midi*	*sètè senk*	*senkè eka* or *senkè kenz*
uitè edmi or *uitè trant*	*uitè mwen senk*	*dezè*	*dizè*

Match and write the correct letter answer below the time

2:10	Midnight	6:15	7:45	11:07
f.	d.	h.	b.	i.
5:27	4:35	8:12	10:38	9:08
e.	g.	a.	j.	c.

a. uitè douz   b. uitè mwen kenz   c. nevè uit   d. minwi   e. senkè vennsèt

f. dezè dis   g. senkè mwen vennsenk   h. sizè eka   i. onzè sèt   j. onzè mwen vennde

Follow the example and write the correct answer in the space provided:

3 +2	10 +40	7 +2	6 +1	12 +10
senk	*senkant*	*nèf*	*sèt*	*vennde*
11 +30	5 +5	15 +15	100 +100	25 +12
karanteyen	*dis*	*trant*	*de san*	*trannsèt*

Fill in the blanks with the correct number word:

en, de, twa, _kat_ , senk, sis, _sèt_ , uit, _nèf_ , dis, _onz_ , _douz_ , trèz, _katòz_ ,kenz,
sèz , disèt, dizuit, _diznèf_ , ven, _venteyen_ , vennde, venntwa, _vennkat_ , vennsenk

How many do you see?

de	*twa*	*senk*
en (youn)	kat	sèt

Months, Days, Seasons and Weather

Vocabulary:

Sunday	dimanch	Monday	lendi	Tuesday	madi
Wednesday	mèkredi	Thursday	jedi	Friday	vandredi
Saturday	samdi	day	jou	week	semenn
month	mwa	season	sezon	January	janvye
February	fevriye	March	mas	April	avril
May	me	June	jen	July	jiyè
August	daou	September	septanm	October	oktòb
November	novanm	December	desanm	Winter	livè
Spring	prentan	Summer	ete	Fall/Autumn	lotòn

The names of months and days are not capitalized in Creole. When giving a specific date, the day comes before the month. The 24th day of January in English is most commonly expressed as *January 24 (January twenty four).* In Creole it is expressed as **24 janvye (vennkat janvye)**. The same is true when substituting numbers for names. The English *01/24/2004* becomes *24/01/2004* in Creole.

As discussed in other lessons, the closer to cities the more the French language increasingly influences Creole. While the above are the true Creole names for months, this is one area that is often confused with French by those who have gone to school. An example is August. In Creole, *August* translates to **daou**. But commonly in the cities, it is pronounced as **out**.

Below is a list of some of the more important Haitian holidays.
January 1 – premye janvye – Independence Day
Januray 2 – de janvye – Forefather's Day
May 18 – dizuit me – Flag Day
November 18 – dizuit novanm – Vètyè Day (an important battle in the war for
                                    Independence

More Vocabualry:

yesterday	yè	tomorrow	demen	day before yesterday	anvan yè
afternoon	apremidi	morning	maten	last (as in last week)	pase
evening	swa	thunder	loray	lightening	zeklè
wet	mouye	dry	sèk	umbrella	parapli
bad weather	move tan	wind	van	breeze	ti van
early	bonè	late	ta	next	pwochenn
hot	cho	cold	frèt	sun	solèy

While there is not a great distinction between seasons in Haiti, they do occur. Weather changes slightly from a little cooler in the winter to warmer in the summer. Most flowers and plants grow year round. Autumn does not have fall colors and falling leaves. The most obvious change in weather is between what is referred to as the *dry season* and the *wet season*, **sezon sechrès** (or simply referred to as sechrès) and **sezon lapli** (rain). These seasons vary depending on the part of the country.

When describing specific weather the word **fè** (makes) is used as the verb.
It is cold – **Li fè frèt**. (It makes cold.)
It is hot. – **Li fè cho**. (It makes hot.)
It will rain. – **Li pral fè lapli**. (It will make rain.)

Li fè is used when the weather is ongoing or in the past or future. For weather conditions taking place in the immediate and for a shorter time, **l'ap fè** is used.

It is raining – **L'ap fè lapli**
It rains a lot in August – **Li fè lapli ampil nan mwa daou**

Worksheet Months, Days, Seasons and Weather

Answer the following questions:

Ki jou ki vini apre mèkredi? _____

Ki jou ki vini anvan madi? _____

Ki jou ki vini anvan samdi? _____

Ki jou ki vini apre dimanch? _____

Ki mwa ki vini apre me? _____

Ki mwa ki vini anvan mars? _____

Ki mwa ki ant jen e daou? _____

Find the days of the week in the Word Jumble. Words may be up, down or across.

m	a	s	n	r	k	v	n	n	i
l	v	a	n	d	r	e	d	i	j
e	i	m	m	s	c	h	d	m	e
n	a	d	i	m	a	n	c	h	k
v	d	i	m	è	k	r	i	n	i
a	i	s		k	s	n	d	j	m
m	a	d	i	r	a	m	n	k	è
c	h	i	d	e	j	d	e	n	r
a	r	j	e	d	a	i	l	c	h
s	a	m	j	i	n	m	a	r	i

Match the sentence with the picture:

a. Li fè frèt.

b. Bonè.

c. L'ap fè lapli.

d. Lotòn.

e. Genyen van.

f. Li fè cho.

g. L'ap fè zeklè

Using the calendars provided, write the answers to the questions in Creole.

janvye

Dimanch	Lendi	Madi	Mèkredi	Jedi	Vandredi	Samdi
				1	2	3
4	5	6	7	8	9	10
11	12	13	14	15	16	17
18	19	20	21	22	23	24
25	26	27	28	29	30	31

novanm

Dimanch	Lendi	Madi	Mèkredi	Jedi	Vandredi	Samdi
	1	2	3	4	5	6
7	8	9	10	11	12	13
14	15	16	17	18	19	20
21	22	23	24	25	26	27
28	29	30				

fevriye

Dimanch	Lendi	Madi	Mèkredi	Jedi	Vandredi	Samdi
1	2	3	4	5	6	7
8	9	10	11	12	13	14
15	16	17	18	19	20	21
22	23	24	25	26	27	28
29						

Kilès mwa ki genyen plis jou? _____

Kilès mwa ki genyen mwens jou? _____

Konbyen jou jedi ki nan mwa fevriye? _____

Ki jou ki dènye jou nan mwa novanm? _____

Janvye komanse ak ki jou? _____

Konbyen jou samdi ki nan mwa janvye? _____

Kilès mwa ki genyen sèlman ventnèf jou?_____

desanm

Dimanch	Lendi	Madi	Mèkredi	Jedi	Vandredi	Samdi
			1	2	3	4
5	6	7	8	9	10	11
12	13	14	15	16	17	18
19	20	21	22	23	24	25
26	27	28	29	30	31	

me

Dimanch	Lendi	Madi	Mèkredi	Jedi	Vandredi	Samdi
						1
2	3	4	5	6	7	8
9	10	11	12	13	14	15
16	17	18	19	20	21	22
23	24	25	26	27	28	29
30	31					

jiyè

Dimanch	Lendi	Madi	Mèkredi	Jedi	Vandredi	Samdi
				1	2	3
4	5	6	7	8	9	10
11	12	13	14	15	16	17
18	19	20	21	22	23	24
25	26	27	28	29	30	31

(assuming northern hemisphere)

Kilès mwa ki fè pi frèt?_____

Kilès mwa ki fè pi cho? _____

Konbyen jou lendi ki nan mwa jiyè? _____

Kilès mwa ki genyen plis jou dimanch? _____

Ki dat dezyèm lendi nan mwa me ye?_____

Ki dat twazyèm mèkredi nan mwa desanm ye? _____

Kilès mwa ki nan sezon prentan? _____

Key Worksheet Months, Days, Seasons and Weather

Answer the following questions:

Ki jou ki vini apre mèkredi? _jedi_

Ki jou ki vini anvan madi? _lendi_

Ki jou ki vini anvan samdi? _vandredi_

Ki jou ki vini apre dimanch? _lendi_

Ki mwa ki vini apre me? _jen_

Ki mwa ki vini anvan mars? _fevriye_

Ki mwa ki ant jen e daou? _jiyè_

m	a	s	n	r	k	v	n	n	i
l	v	a	n	d	r	e	d	i	j
e	i	m	m	s	c	h	d	m	e
n	a	d	i	m	a	n	c	h	k
v	d	i	m	è	k	r	i	n	i
a	i	s		k	s	n	d	j	m
m	a	d	i	r	a	m	n	k	è
c	h	i	d	e	j	d	e	n	r
a	r	j	e	d	a	i	l	c	h
s	a	m	j	i	n	m	a	r	i

:

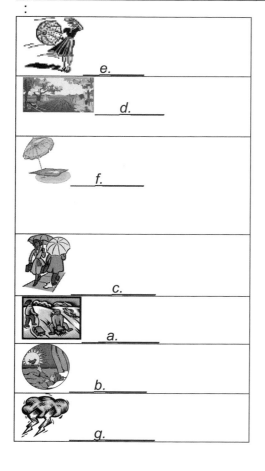

e.

d.

f.

c.

a.

b.

g.

a. Li fè frèt.

b. Bonè.

c. L'ap fè lapli.

d. Lotòn.

e. Genyen van

f. Li fè cho.

g. L'ap fè zeklè

Using the calendars provided, write the answers to the questions in Creole.

janvye

Dimanch	Lendi	Madi	Mèkredi	Jedi	Vandredi	Samdi
				1	2	3
4	5	6	7	8	9	10
11	12	13	14	15	16	17
18	19	20	21	22	23	24
25	26	27	28	29	30	31

novanm

Dimanch	Lendi	Madi	Mèkredi	Jedi	Vandredi	Samdi
	1	2	3	4	5	6
7	8	9	10	11	12	13
14	15	16	17	18	19	20
21	22	23	24	25	26	27
28	29	30				

fevriye

Dimanch	Lendi	Madi	Mèkredi	Jedi	Vandredi	Samdi
1	2	3	4	5	6	7
8	9	10	11	12	13	14
15	16	17	18	19	20	21
22	23	24	25	26	27	28
29						

Kilès mwa ki genyen plis jou? *janvye*

Kilès mwa ki genyen mwens jou? *fevriye*

Konbyen jou jedi ki nan mwa fevriye? *kat*

Ki jou ki dènye jou nan mwa novanm? *madi*

Janvye komanse ak ki jou? *jedi*

Konbyen jou samdi ki nan mwa janvye? *senk*

Kilès mwa ki genyen sèlman ventnèf jou? *fevriye*

desanm

Dimanch	Lendi	Madi	Mèkredi	Jedi	Vandredi	Samdi
			1	2	3	4
5	6	7	8	9	10	11
12	13	14	15	16	17	18
19	20	21	22	23	24	25
26	27	28	29	30	31	

me

Dimanch	Lendi	Madi	Mèkredi	Jedi	Vandredi	Samdi
						1
2	3	4	5	6	7	8
9	10	11	12	13	14	15
16	17	18	19	20	21	22
23	24	25	26	27	28	29
30	31					

jiyè

Dimanch	Lendi	Madi	Mèkredi	Jedi	Vandredi	Samdi
				1	2	3
4	5	6	7	8	9	10
11	12	13	14	15	16	17
18	19	20	21	22	23	24
25	26	27	28	29	30	31

Kilès mwa ki fè pi frèt? *desanm*

Kilès mwa ki fè pi cho? *jiyè*

Konbyen jou lendi ki nan mwa jiyè? *kat*

Kilès mwa ki genyen plis jou dimanch? *me*

Ki dat dezyèm lendi nan mwa me ye? *dis me*

Ki dat twazyèm mèkredi nan mwa desanm ye? *kenz desanm*

Kilès mwa ki nan sezon prentan? *me*

Colors

black	nwa		orange	jòn abriko
white	blan		red	wouj
gray	gri		pink	woz
brown	mawon		burgandy	wouj grena
beige	kaki		purple	mov
ivory	krèm		silver	ajante
blue	ble		gold	dore
navy blue	ble maren		stripes	a bawo
light (sky) blue	ble syèl		plaid	a kawo
green	vèt		variegated	nyanse
yellow	jòn		light (pale)	pal
bright yellow	jòn sitwon		dark	fonse

Colors are adjectives and therefore follow the noun they are describing.

Rad la wouj. *The garment is red.*
Chwal la nwa. *The horse is black.*
Li mov fonse. *It is dark purple.*
Pòt ble a fèmen. *The blue door is closed.*

Interesting notes:

In rural Haiti, many people refer to *greens* as *blue*. Most shades of green are not distinguished; they are simply called blue.

When referring to *gray hair* do not say **gri** (*gray*). It is always called *white hair* or **cheve blan**. **Gri** is also the word for *drunk* because it is thought that a drunken person turns shades of gray.

Worksheet Colors

Write the color(s) of the real life object below the picture:

fig	pye bwa	frèz
zoranj	solèy	bwokoli
elefan	berejen	tonton nèj
zèb	kawòt	kokoye

Read the following conversation aloud and then translate below, using the *Creole Made Easy* dictionary if necessary:

Lenn nan bèl. Gade tout koulè yo. Li genyen anpil koulè. Li sanble yon lakansyèl. Mwen wè woz, ble, jòn sitwon, wouj, vèt, mov, e jòn abriko. Men, gade, lenn nan genyen de bò. Bò sa a genyen tout koulè, men lòt bò a genyen kat koulè. Li a kawo, tou. Koulè bò sa a ble pal, woz, wouj fonse e mov. Medam yo ap koud yon trè bèl lenn.

_____
_____
_____
_____
_____
_____
_____
_____
_____
_____
_____

Complete the sentence below and then translate it:

Cheve grann nan _____.

_____

Key Worksheet Colors

Write the correct color(s) of the real life object underneath the picture:

jòn	*vèt*	*wouj*
jòn abriko	*jòn sitwon*	*vèt*
gri	*mov*	*blan*
blan e nwa	*jòn abriko*	*mawon* (or *mawon e blan*)

Read the following conversation aloud and then translate below, using the *Creole Made Easy* dictionary if necessary:

 Lenn nan bèl. Gade tout koulè yo. Li genyen anpil koulè. Li sanble yon lakansyèl. Mwen wè woz, ble, jòn sitwon, wouj, vèt, mov, e jòn abriko. Men, gade, lenn nan genyen de bò. Bò sa a genyen tout koulè, men lòt bò a genyen kat koulè. Li a kawo, tou. Koulè bò sa a yo ble pal, woz, wouj fonse e mov. Medam yo ap koud yon trè bèl lenn.

The blanket is pretty. Look at all the colors. It has many colors. It looks like a rainbow. I see pink, blue, bright yellow, red, green, purple, and orange. But look, the blanket has two sides. This side has all colors, but the other side has four colors. It is plaid, too. The colors on this side are light blue, pink, dark red, and purple. The ladies are sewing a very pretty blanket.

 Cheve grann nan _blan_ .

The grandmother's hair is white.

Family and Friends

There is a proverb in Haiti that says *"Bonjou se paspò ou"* or *"Hello is your passport."* It is considered very impolite to enter a room or pass someone you know (even nominally) on the street without saying **Bonjou** or **Bonswa**. Usually the one doing the entering or approaching is the one to begin the greeting.

It is also proper to kiss one another on the cheek. Knowing when to expect a kiss and when not is sometimes a problem to the newcomer. In general, man to woman, woman to woman kiss on the cheeks if they know each other or are related. Man to man shake hands. Children, however, may kiss an adult even if it is the first meeting.

Because the word for love and like are the same in Creole, **renmen**, distinguishing what is meant can also be a problem to the newcomer. **Mwen renmen ou** can mean **I like you** or **I love you** depending on the context. However, **mwen renmen avèk ou** means **I am in love with you.**

One of the most important holidays for families in Haiti is New Year's Day. This is the day to visit parents and family. This is the time that most gift exchanges occur. The day is supposed to begin with a bowl of pumpkin soup to assure good fortune throughout the new year.

Vocabulary:

grandfather	granpapa		baby	bebe
grandmother	grann		grandchild	pitit pitit
father	papa		nickname	ti non
mother	manman		step-father	bòpè
son	pitit gason		step-mother	bèlmè
daughter	pitit fi		niece	nyès
sister	sè		nephew	neve
brother	frè		friend	zanmi
little (younger) sister	ti sè		wife	madanm
little (younger)brother	ti frè		husband	mari
older/oldest	pi gran		son-in-law	bòfis
child/children	pitit		daughter-in-law	bèlfi
the children	pitit yo			

father-in-law	bòpè
mother-in-law	bèlmè
brother-in-law	bòfrè
sister-in-law	bèlsè
godfather	parenn
godmother	marenn
aunt	matant
uncle	tonton
cousin (male)	kouzen
cousin (female)	kouzin
fiance(e)	fiyanse
family	fanmi
to meet	fè konnesans

Worksheet for Family and Friends

Read each conversation aloud and then translate it below.

Stephanie: "Mwen prale kay granpapa mwen. Kouzin mwen, Nancy, la. Nou va manje ansanm."

Lisa: "Mwen bezwen vizite matant mwen jodi a. Lè mwen fini, eske ou vle vini la kay mwen ak kouzin ou?"

Stephanie: "Wi, sa ta bon. Pètèt sè ou, Anne, kapab vini."

Lisa: Anne ap vizite bòpè nou. Li pa kapab vini."

Stephanie: "Dakò, mwen va wè ou pita."

_____

_____

_____

_____

_____

_____

_____

_____

_____

_____

Robert: "Bonjou Pepe. Eske ou konnen sè mwen? Li rele Jeanette."

Pepe: "Bonjou, Robert. Non, mwen poko fè konnensans sè ou."

Robert: "Janjan, sa se Pierre, zanmi mwen."

Jeanette: Bonjou, Pierre, mwen kontan fè konnesans ou."

Pepe: "Mwen kontan fè konnesans pa ou, tou. Eske Janjan se ti non ou?"

Jeanette: "Wi, se ti non mwen.

Pepe: "Rele mwen Pepe si ou vle. Pepe se ti non pa mwen."

_____

_____

_____

_____

_____

_____

_____

_____

_____

Write the word or words under the picture that matche(s) the person.

kouzen, frè/sè, granpapa, manman, grann/pitit pitit, fanmi, pitit fi,
papa/pitit gason, granpapa/pitit pitit

Family Tree

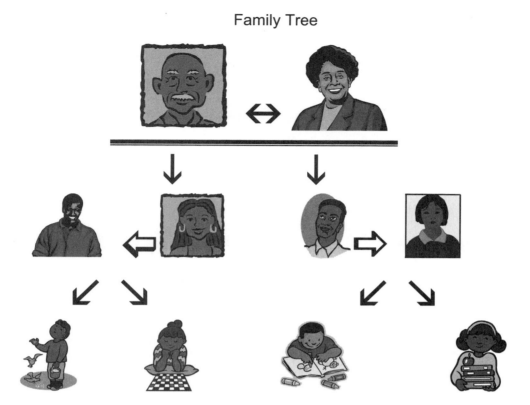

Fill in the proper relationship based on the above family tree. The first one is done as an example.

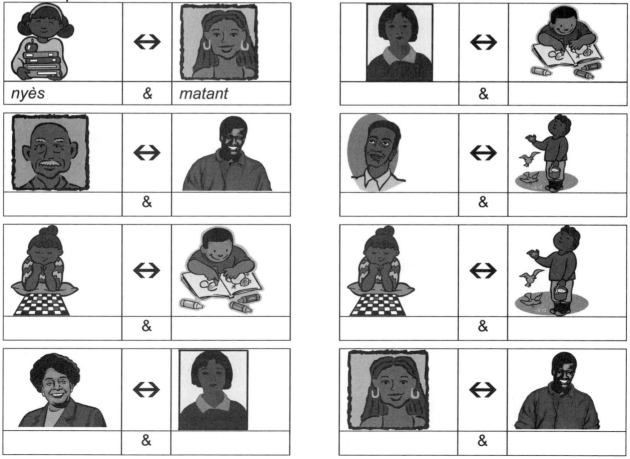

| nyès | & | matant |

Key Worksheet Family and Friends

Conversations:

Stephanie: "I am going to my grandfather's house. My cousin, Nancy, is there. We are going to eat together."

Lisa: "I need to visit my aunt today. When I am done, do you want to come to my house with your cousin?"

Stephanie: "Yes, that would be nice. Maybe your sister, Anne, can come.

Lisa: Anne is visiting our stepfather today. She cannot come."

Stephanie: "Ok, I will see you later."

Robert: "Hello, Pepe. Do you know my sister? Her name is Jeanette?" (She is called Jeanette.)

Pepe: "Hello, Robert. No, I do not yet know your sister."

Robert: "Janjan, this is Pierre, my friend."

Jeanette: "Hello, Pierre, I am happy to meet you."

Pepe: "I am happy to meet you, too. Is Janjan your nickname?"

Jeanette: "Yes, Perre, it is my nickname."

Pepe: "Call me Pepe if you like. Pepe is my nickname."

Write the word or words under the picture that matche(s) the person.

pitit fi	manman	kouzen
granpapa/pitit pitit	papa/pitit gason	gran/pitit pitit
frè/sè	granpapa	fanmi

Family Tree – relationships:

nyès	matant		manman	pitit gason
bòpè	bòfis		tonton	neve
kouzin	kouzen		sè	frè
bèlme	bèlfi		madanm	mari

Marketplace and Food

Market and Shopping

Many of the best foods in Haiti are found in the market place. Fresh fruits, vegetables, grains like rice and corn meal, and a variety of other things can be bartered for in the open market. The **machann** (*merchant/vendor*) expects bartering and always asks a higher price than expected. The buyer is expected to make a lower counter-offer and agree on a price between the two. This process increases social interaction and when done with respect it is a healthy part of daily life in Haiti.

Marketplace vocabulary:

agree, accept, ok	dakò	last (best) price	dènye pri
bargain to	machande	merchandise	machandiz
a bargain	bon pri	merchant/vendor	machann
can, tin, measure	mamit	money	kòb
dozen	douzèn	need	bezwen
each	chak	sell	vann
bonus	degi	the market place	mache
how much	konbyen	too expensive	twò chè
inexpensive	pa chè	too much	twòp

Note the word **degi** *(bonus)* above. If you buy several things from a merchant ask for your **degi**, as part of the social exchange. It is common practice to add a little to the pile or throw in an extra piece of fruit if you are buying a lot. A **mamit** or *can* is often used as a measuring device. It is usually a gallon can which is filled to the top or even above. Typically, however, as much as can be put into the can is one **mamit**. Sometimes items like potatoes, sweet potatoes, and plantain are sold in *piles* or *mounds* (**pil**) and priced by the pile. Fruits are often sold by the dozen and many vegetables are sold by the piece.

While many grocery stores carry quite a variety of items, specialty stores also exist. Below is a list of vocabulary words for the various types of stores.

Magazen –a store like a hardware store or fabric store.. This is not usually used to refer to a grocery store (makèt).

Makèt –a grocery store. Do not confuse this with the open market (**mache**).

Mache –an open market, where almost anything can be purchased and bartering is a way of life. Rural areas all have a **jou mache**, or *market day* each week.

Boutik – a small, general store that sells a wide variety of items including some foods.

Famasi –a pharmacy for medicines and medical items.

Boulanjri –a bakery. Fresh breads and pastries are best when purchased from a bakery. A few bakeries supply **bagèt** (French bread) to the local grocery stores.

Bouchri –a butcher shop. Meat is often cut and prepared on request. The more rural the butcher shop, the less choice there is in types of cuts. For example in small towns often the choices are **filè** (tenderloin, filet mignon), **fo filè** (loin), **woti** –*roast* (all other cuts) or **vyann moulen** (ground meat).

Libreri –a bookstore. They often sell school related supplies as well as books and newspapers.

Ponp, **ponp gazolin** –a gas station.

Restoran –a restaurant.

Survival sentences for the market (mache)

Do you sell ......? **Eske ou vann....?**
How much is it/are they? **Konbyen li/yo ye?**
That's too much.   **Sa se twòp.**
It is too expensive.   **Li twò chè.**
I want one dozen? **Mwen vle yon douzèn.**
Where can I buy....? **Ki kote mwen kapab achte....?**
I will give/pay you..... **Mwen va ba ou......?**
No, thank you, I don't need those.* **Non mesi, mwen pa bezwen sa yo.**
I don't have any money. **Mwen pa genyen kòb.**
I want to buy..... **Mwen vle achte....**
Excuse me, I am in a hurry. **Eskize, mwen prese. (Padon, mwen prese.)**

*Note: One is always offered produce and other items when shopping in the open market. Some merchants are very pushy. Instead of saying I don't need that or I don't want that, sometimes explaining that "*I have that already*" – **Mwen genyen sa deja**" will convince the person that you will not be buying any more now.

Food Vocabulary

Meats and seafoods:

bacon	bekonn	meatball	boulèt
beef	bèf, vyann bèf	oyster	zwit
brains	sèvèl	pigeon	pijon
chicken	poul	pork	vyann kochon
chicken thigh	kwis poul	poultry	volay
chicken breast	fal poul	rabbit	lapen
codfish, salted/dried	mori	roast	woti
conch	lanbi	salami	salami
crab	krab	salmon	somon
crayfish/crawfish	kribich	sardine	sadin
duck	kanna	sausage	sosis
fish	pwason	seafood	bèt lanmè
goat	kabrit	shrimp	ekrevis
ground beef	vyann moulen	skin	po
guinea fowl	pentad	snapper	sad
ham	janbon	sole	sòl
hamburger	anbègè	steak	estèk
dried smoked herring	aran, aransò	tongue	lang
hot dog	hòt dòg, sosis hòt dòg	tripe	trip
lamb	vyann mouton	tuna	ton
liver	fwa	turkey	koden
lobster	woma	turtle	tòti

Note: The word for meat is **vyann**. Most meats are described by using the word **vyann** and adding the name of the animal. *Pork* is **vyann kochon**, *beef* becomes **vyann bèf**, and *goat* is **vyann kabrit**. However, animals usually cooked whole, such as chicken, fish and rabbit omit the word **vyann** (meat). *Chicken* is **poul** and *fish* is **pwason**.

Dairy:

butter	bè	margarine	magarin
cheese	fwomaj	milk	lèt
cream	krèm lèt	milk, clotted	lèt kaye
egg	ze	milk, evaporated	lèt vapore
ice cream	krèm	sherbet, sorbet	sòbè

Spices, condiments and flavorings:

catsup/ketchup	sòs tomat, katchòp	parsley	pèsi
cinnamon	kanèl	peanut butter	manba
clove	jiwòf	peanut butter (spicy)	manba pike
cocoa	poud kakawo	pepper (black)	pwav
garlic	lay	pickle	kònichon
ginger	jenjanm	relish (cabbage, hot)	pikliz
honey	siwo myèl	sage	souj
jam	konfiti	salt	sèl
jelly	jele	sea salt	gwo sèl
mayonnaise	mayonèz	seasoning	epis
mint, peppermint	mant	spearmint	tibonm
mustard	moutad	spice	epis
nutmeg	miskad	syrup	siwo
oil	lwil	thyme	ten
olive	zoliv	tomato paste	pat tomat
olive oil	lwildoliv	vanilla	vani, esans
oregano	oregano	vinegar	vinèg

Breads, pasta and grains:

bread	pen	muffin	ponmkèt
bread (loaf) *	pen tranche	oatmeal	avwan
bulgur/cracked wheat	ble	popcorn	mayi pèt pèt
cassava bread	kasav	rice	diri
cornmeal	mayi moulen	roll	pen won
crescent roll	kwasan	spaghetti	espageti
flour	farin	vermicelli	vèmisèl
French bread	bagèt	wheat	ble
macaroni	makawoni	whole wheat flour	farin ble
millet	pitimi	yeast	leven

* Note: A loaf of *sliced bread* is referred to as **pen tranche**, as other forms of bread are not sliced.

Fruits, nuts and vegetables:

almond	zanmann	mango	mango
apple	ponm	manioc	manyòk
apricot	abriko	melon	melon
asparagus	aspèj	nut	nwa
avocado	zaboka	okra	kalalou, gonbo
banana	fig. fig mi	olive	zoliv
bean	pwa	onion	zonyon
beet	bètwouj	orange	zoranj
breadfruit	lam veritab	palm heart	chou palmis
broccoli	bwokoli	papaya	papay
butterbean	pwa bè	passionfruit	grenadya, grenadin
cabbage	chou	pea	pwa frans
cantaloupe	kantaloup	peanut	pistach
carrot	kawòt	pepper (hot)	piman pike
casaba melon	melon frans	pimento	piman dous
cashew	nwa kajou	pineapple	zannanna
cauliflower	chouflè	plantain	bannann
celery	seleri	potato	pomdetè
chayote squash	militon	produce (vegetables)	legim
cherry	seriz	pumpkin	joumou
coconut	kokoye	radish	radi
corn	mayi	raisin	rezen sèk
corn on the cob	mayi ole	raspberry	franbwaz
cucumber	konkonm	shaddock	chadèk
eggplant	berejèn	shallot	echalòt
fruit	fwi	sour orange *	zoranj si
grape	rezen	soursop	kowosòl
grapefruit	panplemous	spinach	zepina
green beans	pwa tann	squash	eskwash, koujèt
green pea	pwa frans	strawberry	frèz
green pepper	piman dous	string bean	pwa tann
guava	gwayav	sweet potato	patat
kidney bean	pwa wouj	tamarind	tamaren
leek	pwawo	tangerine	mandarin
lemon	limon	tomato	tomat
lentil	lantiy	turnip	nave
lettuce	leti	vegetable	legim
lima bean	pwa souch	watermelon	melon dlo
lime	sitwon	yam	yanm
mamey	zabriko		

*Note: The sour orange found in Haiti is used for marinating meat to make it more tender. It also has a medicinal use. When rubbed onto a sprain or bruise the area is said to heal much more quickly.

Beverages:

beer	byè	tea	te
coffee	kafe	tea, herbal	tizan
drink	bwason	tea, hot	te cho
fruit punch	fwitponch	tonic water	tonik
hot chocolate	chokola nan lèt cho	water	dlo
ice	glas	water, bottled	dlo kiligann, dlo nan boutey
iced, cold	glase	water, purified	dlo distile
iced tea	te glase	Coca cola	koka
juice*	ji	Pepsi cola	pepsi
milk	lèt	Fruit Champagne	kola
mineral water	dlo mineral	Ginger Ale	kola jenjanm
rum	wonm	Grape Soda	kola rezen
rum punch	wonmponch	Orange Soda	kola zoranj

*Note: To request a specific fruit juice add the name of the fruit after "**ji**."

orange juice – **ji zoranj**   *limeade* – **ji sitwon**

papaya juice – **ji papay**   *passion fruit juice* – **ji grenadya**

Sweets and desserts:

cake	gato	ice cream	krèm
candy (hard)	sirèt	Jello	jelo
candy (praline)*	tablèt	muffin	ponmkèt
candy (fudge)*	dous	pie	tat
chewing gum	chiklèt	sherbet, sorbet	sòbè
chocolate	chokola	sugar	sik
cookie	bonbon	sugar, powdered	sik a glase, sik an poud
cupcake	kokonèt, pomkèt	sugar, brown/raw	sik wouj
dessert	desè	sweet(s)	dous
guava paste	pat gwayav	syrup	siwo
honey	siwo myèl	tart (fruit)	tat

* Note: Clarification of types of candy:

A **sirèt** is the equivalent of a *hard candy* wrapped in paper. There is also a **mant**, a softer peppermint candy (often wrapped in paper).

Dous is a *fudge* like candy made from sugar and brown sugar poured onto a sheet and cut into pieces.

Tablèt is a *praline* with nuts (usually peanuts or cashews) or coconut and is shaped into an individual sized round piece of candy.

Miscellaneous:

alcohol	alkòl	leftovers	manje dòmi
bone	zo	mashed potatoes	ponmdetè pire
chips	papita	milk, powdered	lèt an poud
corn flakes	kònfleks	mushroom	champiyon
cornmeal mush	mayi moulen	mushroom (small black variety)	djondjon
cornmeal pudding	akasan	oatmeal, cooked	avwan, labouyi avwan
cracker	biswit sèk	pancake	krèp
dumpling	bòy, doumbrèy	pizza	pitza
egg, hard boiled	ze bouyi	plantain chips	papita
egg, fried	ze fri	plantain slices fried	bannann peze
egg, poached	ze poche	rice and beans	diri kole ak pwa
egg, scrambled	ze bwouye, zebat	rice and bean sauce	diri ak sòs pwa
egg, soft boiled	ze alakòk	rice, black mushroom	diri djondjon
fat	grès	salad	salad
food	manje	sandwich	sandwich
French fries	ponmdetè fri	sauce	sòs
French toast	pen pèdi	shortening	mantèg
fritter	marinad	snack	soloba
fritter (with malanga)	akra	snowcone	fresko
gravy	sòs	soup	soup
grease	grès	stew	bouyon
lard	mantèg	toast	pen griye

Worksheet for Marketplace and Food

Pick the right one:

Mwen vle achte

- ❑ I need some
- ❑ I want to buy
- ❑ I am going
- ❑ Take me to

Li twò chè

- ❑ It is pretty
- ❑ I want one
- ❑ She is selling
- ❑ It is too expensive

Mwen genyen sa deja

- ❑ I have that already
- ❑ I don't need any
- ❑ Do you have
- ❑ Where can I buy

Match the stores:

___ Marketplace	a. famasi
___ Bookstore	b. magazen
___ Butcher shop	c. boulanjri
___ Gas station	d. makèt
___ Store (like a fabric shop)	e. ponp
___ Pharmacy	f. restoran
___ Grocery store	g. mache
___ Bakery	h. libreri
___ Restaurant	i. bouchri

Match the item you wish to buy with the correct place to find it:

_____	vyann moulen	a. mache
_____	gazolin	b. libreri
_____	bagèt (pen)	c. bouchri
_____	bè	d. boulanjri
_____	moso twal	e. ponp
_____	sitwon	f. makèt
_____	liv	g. magazen

Write the Creole name below the picture:

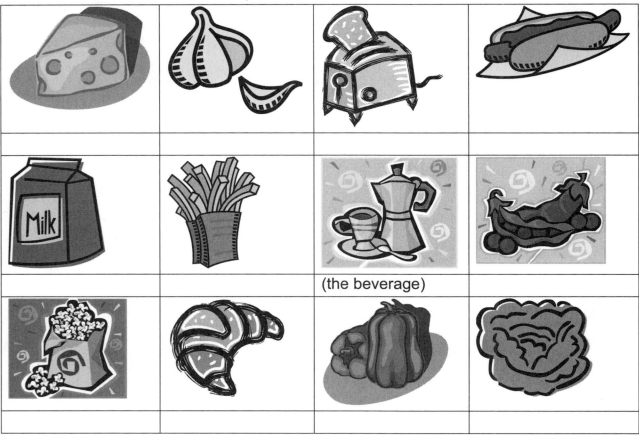

(the beverage)

Key for worksheet for Marketplace and Food

Pick the right one:
Mwen vle achte
☐ I need some
☒ *I want to buy*
☐ I am going
☐ Take me to

Li twò chè
☐ It is pretty
☐ I want one
☐ She is selling
☒ *It is too expensive*

Mwen genyen sa deja
☒ *I have that already*
☐ I don't need any
☐ Do you have
☐ Where can I buy

Match the stores:

_g._	Marketplace	a. famasi
_h._	Bookstore	b. magazen
_i._	Butcher shop	c. boulanjri
_e._	Gas station	d. makèt
_b._	Store (like a fabric shop)	e. ponp
_a._	Pharmacy	f. restoran
_d._	Grocery store	g. mache
_c._	Bakery	h. libreri
_f._	Restaurant	i. bouchri

Match the item you wish to buy with the correct place to find it:

_c._	vyann moulen	a. mache	
_e._	gazolin	b. libreri	
_d._	bagèt (pen)	c. bouchri	
_f._	bè	d. boulanjri	
_g._	moso twal	e. ponp	
_a._	sitwon	f. makèt	
_b._	liv	g. magazen	

Write the Creole name below the picture:

fwomaj	lay	pen griye	hòt dòg, sosis hòt dòg
lèt	ponmdetè fri	kafe	pwa frans
mayi pèt pèt	kwasan	piman dous	leti

Around the House

This unit is intended to teach household related vocabualry.
Household terms and items:

alarm clock	revèy	lampshade	abajou
bath	ben, beny	laundry	lesiv
bathtub	benywa	match	alimèt
bed	kabann	mirror	glas, miwa
bed sheets	dra	mop	mòp
bedspread	kouvreli	napkin	sèvyèt
bench, stool	ban	oven	fou
blanket	lenn	pantry	gad manje
chair	chèz	pillow	zorye
clock	òlòj, pandil	pillow case	tèt zorye
clothes hanger	sèso	radio	radyo
cradle	bèso	refrigerator	frijidè
cupboard/cabinet	bifèt	rug	tapi
curtain	rido	shower	douch
cushion	kousen	sink (bathroom)	lavabo
dishpan, wash basin	kivèt	sink (kitchen)	evye
dirt, krud	kras	sink strainer	krepin
dirty	sal	sofa, couch	divan
door	pòt	stain	tach
dust	pousyè	stairs	eskalye
flashlight	flach	starch	lanmidon
floor	atè	table	tab
freezer	frizè	tablecloth	nap
furniture	mèb	telephone	telefòn
hallway	koulwa	television	televizyon
housekeeper/maid	bòn	trash can	poubèl
iron (noun)	fè	toilet	watè
ironing board	planchèt	vase	po
ladder	nechèl	wall	mi
lamp/light	limyè	window	fenèt

Household tasks:

change the sheets	chanje dra yo	make the bed(s)	fè kabann nan (yo)
clean	netwaye	set the table	mete kouvè
to cook	kwit	sweep*	bale
to dry	seche	to telephone	telefonnen
to dust	siye, siye pousyè	turn on	ouvri, pase
to hang up	kwoke	wash	lave
to iron	repase	wash dishes	lave vèsèl
to light	limen	wash the floor	pase mòp

* *Sweep the floor"* may be said as "**Pase bale**". It is more common to ask for a specific room or place to be swept. "*Sweep the kitchen*" becomes "**Bale kizin nan.**"

Kitchen related items:

bottle	boutèy	jar	bokal
bottle opener	kle kola	kettle	bonm
cake pan	plato pou gato	knife	kouto
can	mamit	mill/grinder	moulen
coffee pot	kafetyè	mixing bowl	bòl
cookie sheet	plato pou bonbon	mortar/pestle	pilon, manch pilon
cup	tas	pitcher	po
dishes	vèsèl	place setting	kouvè
dish towel	tòchon	plate	asyèt
drinking glass	vè	pot, saucepan	kastwòl
egg beater	batèz	propane gas*	gaz
fork	fouchèt	sharp knife	kouto file
frying pan	pwèl	spoon	kiyè
funnel	antònwa	steel wool	paydefè
grate (v)	graje, rape	strainer	paswa
grater	graj	tin cup	gode

*Note: Much of rural Haiti's cooking is done with charcoal or wood. Homes with ovens use propane gas, available in 25# or 100# tanks.

Common cooking terms and foods

add	ajoute	mix	melanje
bake	kwit nan fou	peel	kale
beat	bat	raw	kri
boil	bouyi	remove	wetire
cover	kouvri	soak	tranpe
cut	koupe	spice, seasoning	epis
dice	tchake	spicy hot	pike
fry	fri	squeeze	prije
iced	glase	stir	brase
marinate	tranpe	strain	koule, pase nan paswa

Measurements

cup	tas	one & a half cups	tas edmi
half cup	demi tas	tablespoon	gwo kiyè
quarter cup	ka tas	teaspoon	(ti) kiyè
one & a quarter cup	tas eka	dash/a little	ti kras

Rooms of the house:

bathroom	kabinè, saldeben	kitchen	kizin
bedroom	chanm	living room	salon
closet	amwa *	office	biwo
dining room	salamanje	storeroom	depo

Amwa is the word for *wardrobe*, a piece of furniture made for storing clothes. Closets as separate rooms are rare in rural homes and a specific word for such does not exist in the Creole language.

Clothing terms and items:

blouse	kòsay	shirt	chemiz
bra	soutyen	shoes	soulye
cap, baseball cap	kaskèt	shorts	pantalon kout
clothes	rad	skirt	jip
coat	palto	slip	jipon
collar	kòl	slippers	pantouf
cuff	pwaye	socks	chosèt
dress	wòb	stockings, hose	ba
gloves	gan	suit (men's)	kostim
handkerchief	mouchwa	suit coat	vès
hat	chapo	swimsuit	kostimdeben
jacket (men's)	vès	swim trunks	chòtdeben
nightgown	wòbdenwi	tie, necktie	kravat
pajamas	pijama	t-shirt	mayo
pants	pantalon	underpants (men's)	kalson
robe, bathrobe	wòbdeben	underpants (panties)	kilòt
scarf	foula	undershirt	chemizèt

Sewing terms:

bobbin	bobin	sewing	kouti
button	bouton	to sew	koud
to button	boutonnen	sewing machine	machin a koud
cloth	twal	tailor	tayè
hem	woulèt	thimble	de
to hem	bay woulèt	thread	fil
needle	zegwi	to thread	file
pattern	patwon	torn	chire
seamstress	koutriyèz	zipper	zip

Worksheet for Around the House

Fill in the blank with correct room.

_____   _____

_____   _____

Translate into Creole:

I need to do laundry today.

_____

Please sweep the bedroom floor.

_____

Please clean the bathroom.

_____

I will iron the clothes when I finish making the bed.

_____

After you wash the clothes, they need to dry before you iron them.

_____

Kettly will make the beds.

_____

The milk is in the refrigerator.

_____

Light the stove with a match.

_____

The windows are dirty.

_____

Housecleaning: Select the best room for items below and write the name of the item below the room.

kafetyè, nap, frizè, divan, kabann, vès, pwèl, kravat, rad, lavabo, lenn, zorye, evye, televizyon, watè, kastwòl, wòb, kouvè, asyèt, epis, wòbdenwi, tab, pantouf, frigidè, kivèt, dra, chèz, sèvyèt, fou, douch, kòsay, soulye, fouchèt, vesèl, paydefè, tapi, tèt zorye, benywa, revèy, kouvreli, sèso, glas

Translate the recipe into Creole:

Butter Cookies

Beat 1 cup butter with one egg. Add 2 ¼ cups flour. Stir all together. Add ½ cup sugar. Put in ½ teaspoon vanilla. Mix well. Put it by spoonfuls onto a cookie sheet.

Bake them in the oven for 12 minutes or until they take color.

Key Worksheet Around the House

Fill in the blank with the correct room.

salamanje	*sal deben* or *kabinè*
salon	*chanm*

Translate into Creole:

I need to do laundry today.

Mwen bezwen fè lesiv jodi a.

Please sweep the bedroom floor.

Tanpri, bale chanm nan.

Please clean the bathroom.

Tanpri, netwaye saldeben an. (kabinè a)

I will iron the clothes when I finish making the bed.

Mwen pral repase rad yo lè mwen fini fè kabann nan.

After you wash the clothes, they need to dry before you iron them.

Aprè ou lave rad yo, yo bezwen seche anvan ou repase yo.

Kettly will make the beds.

Kettly pral fè kabann yo.

The milk is in the refrigerator.

Lèt la nan frigidè a.

Light the stove with a match.

Limen fou a avèk yon alimèt.

The windows are dirty.

Fenèt yo sal.

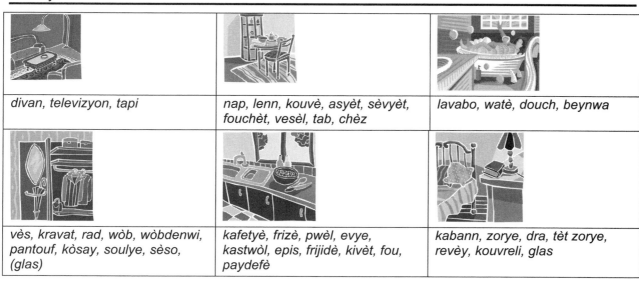

divan, televizyon, tapi	*nap, lenn, kouvè, asyèt, sèvyèt, fouchèt, vesèl, tab, chèz*	*lavabo, watè, douch, beynwa*
vès, kravat, rad, wòb, wòbdenwi, pantouf, kòsay, soulye, sèso, (glas)	*kafetyè, frizè, pwèl, evye, kastwòl, epis, frijidè, kivèt, fou, paydefè*	*kabann, zorye, dra, tèt zorye, revèy, kouvreli, glas*

Translate the recipe into Creole:

Butter Cookies

Beat 1 cup butter with one egg. Add 2 ¼ cups flour. Stir all together. Add ½ cup sugar. Put in ½ teaspoon vanilla. Mix well. Put it by spoonfuls onto a cookie sheet.

Bake them in the oven for 12 minutes or until they take color.

Bonbon Bè

Bat yon tas bè avèk yon zè. Ajoute 2 tas eka farin. Brase tout ansanm. Ajoute yon demi tas sik. Mete yon demi kiyè vani (esans). Melange tout byen. Mete li pa kiye sou yon plato bonbon. Kwit yo nan fou pou douz minit oubyen jouk yo pran koulè.

Health and Medicine

Describing an illness is often difficult even when being done in one's native tongue. Trying to do so in a foreign language can be at best very frustrating. The vocabulary and lessons in this chapter are intended to help with medical conversations.

Conditions and ailments:

anemia	anemi	hernia	èni
appendicitis	apenndisit	hives	bouton
arthritis	atrit	hypertension	tensyon wo
asthma	opresyon	hypotension	tensyon ba
bladder infection	enfeksyon blad	indigestion	gonfleman
bloated	gonflè	jaundice	lajònis
colic	kolik	malaria	palidis
diabetes	sik, dyabèt	nausea	vomisman
diarrhea	djare	mumps	malmouton
eczema	egzema	pneumonia	nemoni
heart attack	kriz kadyak	pregnancy	gwosès
heartburn	zègrè	rash	gratèl
heat rash	bouton chalè	tetanus	tetanòs
hemorrhoid	emowoyid	typhoid	tifoyid

The body:

abdomen	vant	liver	fwa
ankle	koud pye	lungs	poumon
arm	bra	mouth	bouch
back	do	muscle	misk, chè
bladder	blad pise	navel	lonbrit
breast	tete, sen	neck	kou
chest	pwatrin, lestomak	nose	nen
ear	zòrèy	palm	pla men
elbow	koud bra	rib	kòt
eye	je, zye*	penis	pati gason
eyelid	po je	shoulder	zepòl
face	figi	spine	rèl do
finger	dwèt	stomach	vant
fingernail	zong	sternum	biskèt
foot	pye	tooth	dan
gall bladder	fyèl	throat	gòj
hair	cheve	toe	zòtèy
hand	men	toenail	zong pye
head	tèt	tongue	lang
heart	kè	vagina	bòbòt, pati fi
hip	ranch	vein	venn
kidney	ren	waist	tay
knee	jenou	wisdom tooth	dan zòrèy
knuckle	jwenti dwèt	womb	matris
leg	janm	wrist	ponyèt

Note: Though it is not a grammatical rule, there is a tendancy to use je for one eye and zye and two eyes.

The vocabulary below is intended to help a non-medical person communicate or understand an ailment or condition. A more complete list of medical related vocabulary can be found at the end of this chapter.

Vocabulary:

abcess	abse	head ache	maltèt, tè fè mal
accident	aksidan	hemorrhage	emoraji
allergic	genyen alèji	hospital	lopital
allergy	alèji	hospitalize	entène
ambulance	anbilans	hurts	fè mal
anesthsia	anestezi	illness	maladi
appetite	apeti	infect	bay maladi
artery (blood vessel)	venn	infectious	atrapan
bandage, band aide	pansman	inflamed	wouj, anfle
belch	rann gaz	instructions	ekspikasyon
bite (n)	kout dan	itch	gratèl
bite (v)	mòde	laboratory	laboratwa
bleeding	senyen	medicine	remèd, medikaman
blood pressure	tansyon	menstrual cycle, period	règ
breathe	respire	nervous	ajite, enève
broken	kase	nurse	enfimyè, mis
bruise	metri	overweight	twò gra
clinic	klinik	pain	doulè
cold (n)	grip	painkiller	remèd pou doulè
cough,	tous	parasite	parazit
cramp	lakranp	patient	malad, pasyan
critical	grav	pregnant	ansent
dehydrated	kò sèch, dezidrate	pull a tooth	rache dan
dentures	atelye	pulmonary	pilmonè, nan poumon
disinfect	dezenfekte	relapse	tonbe malad ankò
doctor	doktè	sanitary napkin	kotèks
doctor's office	biwo doktè, klinik	shot (injection)	piki
dosage, dose	dòz	sick	malad
earache	malzòrèy	sore throat	malgòj
emergency, urgency	ijans	sprain	antòs
examination, exam	egzamen	stomach ache	vent fè mal
examine	egzamine	thermometer	tèmomèt
examine (a patient)	konsilte	to cough	touse
explanation	eksplikasyon	to vomit	rechte, vomi
faint	endispoze	toothache	maldan
fatigue	fatig	turn around	virewon
feeling (n)	sansasyon	undress, take off clothes	dezabiye
fever	lafyèv	urinate	pipi
fill a tooth	plonbe	vomit	vomi
flu	grip	well (not sick)	pa malad
fracture (v)	fractire, kase	wounded, injured	blese
gargle	gagari	x-ray	radyografi

Some helpful phrases:

I have a fever.	Mwen genyen lafyèv.
Do you have a fever?	Eske ou genyen lafyèv?
It hurts.	Li fè mal.
Where does it hurt?	Ki kote li fè mal?
We need a doctor right away!	Nou bezwen yon doktè toutswit!
Does the doctor speak English?	Eske doktè a pale angle?
I am sick.	Mwen malad.
I have a head ache.	Mwen genyen yon maltèt.
I have diarrhea.	Mwen genyen djare.
I have no appetite.	Mwen pa genyen apeti.
I have pain.	Mwen gen doulè.
Do you have pain?	Eske ou genyen doulè?
I have a toothache.	Mwen gen maldan.
I have something in my eye.	Mwen gen yon baygay nan je mwen.
I have indigestion.	Mwen gonfle.
I have my period.	Mwen gen règ mwen.
I vomited.	Mwen te vomi.
I am allergic to that.	Mwen gen alèji ak sa.
She fainted.	Li endispoze.
He is hurt (injured).	Li blese.
It hurts here.	Li fè mal isit.
Do not move him.	Pa deplase li.
I need to buy (some) medicine.	Mwen bezwen achte remèd.
I am a diabetic.	Mwen dyabèt.
There was an accident.	Te genyen yon aksidan.
Please call the nurse.	Tanpri, rele mis la.
Where does it hurt?	Ki kote li fè mal?
Do you have sanitary napkins?	Eske ou genyen kotèks?
Where is the pharmacy?	Ki kote famasi a ye?
Do you have a bandage?	Eske ou genyen yon pansman?
Take 2 tablets 3 times a day.	Bwè de gren twa fwa pa jou.
Take 1 teaspoon once daily.	Bwè yon ti kiyè yon fwa pa jou.
Apply topically each morning and night.	Pase sou po chak maten e swa.

Note: To say "it hurts" in Creole, one says "li fè mal" or literally, "it makes bad."
Note: Genyen (have) may be shorten to gen. Both forms are used above, but they are interchangeable.

A *general practitioner* is a **doktè**. Other specialist are listed below:

cardiologist	kadyològ, doktè kè	optometrist	doktè je
dentist	dantis	orthopedist	òtopedis, doktè zo
gynecologist	doktè fanm	pediatrician	pedyat, doktè timoun
neurologist	doktè niwoloji	podiatrist	doktè pye
obstetrician	doktè fanm	surgeon	chirijyen

Note: In rural areas, the more common way to refer to a specialist is to say "doktè" and then state the area of specialty. For example: An *orthopedist* might be known as an **òtopedis** near a city, but as a **doktè zo** (*bone doctor*) in more rural areas.

Worksheet Health and Medicine

Select the Creole translation for the English sentence:

I need a doctor.
- ◯   Mwen bezwen yon enfimyè.
- ◯   Mwen genyen maltèt
- ◯   Mwen bezwen yon doktè.

Her tooth hurts.
- ◯   Bra li kase.
- ◯   Dan li fè mal.
- ◯   Li genyen lafyèv.

Where is the hospital?
- ◯   Ki kote lopital la ye?
- ◯   Ki kote ou prale?
- ◯   Ki lès ki dokè a?

Does she have fever?
- ◯   Eske ou genyen yon malgòj?
- ◯   Eske li fè mal?
- ◯   Eske li genyen lafyèv?

Label the body parts with the correct Creole word:

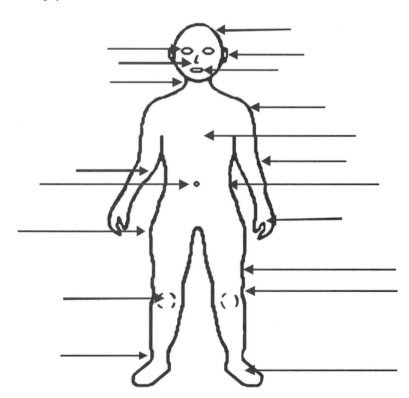

Match the picture with the best sentence. Then translate the sentence.

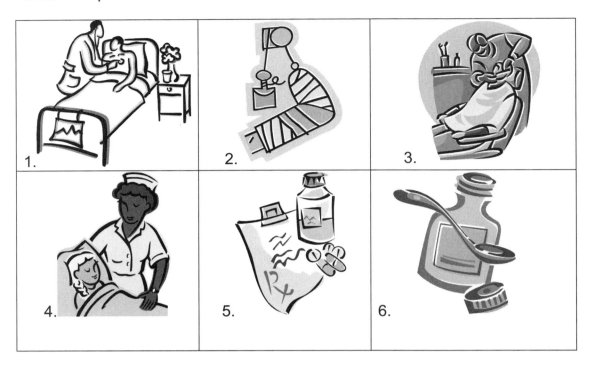

_____ Pye mwen kase nan yon aksidan.

_____

_____ Doktè a ap egzamine malad la.

_____

_____ Doktè a di pou timoun nan bwe yon kiye nan remèd la chak jou.

_____

_____ Dantis la ap plonbe yon dan.

_____

_____ Mis la ap swen timoun nan.

_____

_____ Mwen bezwen yon famasi pou m' achete remèd la.

_____

Key Worksheet Health and Medicine

Select the Creole translation for the English sentence:
I need a doctor.
- ○   Mwen bezwen yon enfimyè.
- ○   Mwen genyen maltèt
- ●   Mwen bezwen yon doktè.

Her tooth hurts.
- ○   Bra li kase.
- ●   Dan li fè mal.
- ○   Li genyen lafyèv.

Where is the hospital?
- ●   Ki kote lopital la ye?.
- ○   Ki kote ou prale?
- ○   Ki lès ki dokè a?

Does she have fever?
- ○   Eske ou genyen yon malgòj?
- ○   Eske li fè mal?
- ●   Eske li genyen lafyèv?

Label the body parts with the correct Creole word:

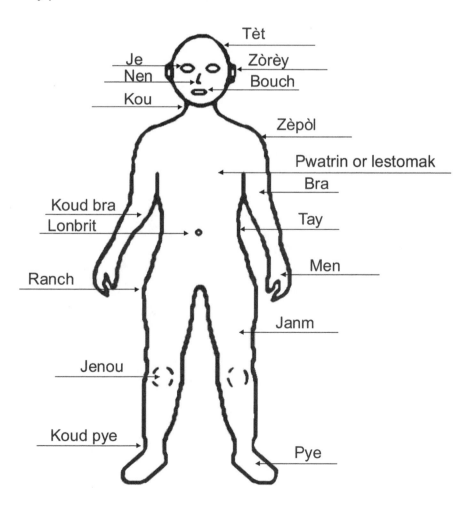

Match the picture with the best sentence. Then translate the sentence.

1.	2.	3.
4.	5.	6.

2. Pye mwen kase nan yon aksidan.
My foot broke in an accident.

1. Doktè a ap egzamine malad la.
The doctor is examining the patient.

6. Doktè a di pou timoun nan bwe yon kiye remèd chak jou.
The doctor said for the child to drink one spoon of medicine each day.

3. Dantis la ap plonbe yon dan.
The dentist is filling a tooth.

4. Mis la ap ede timoun nan.
The nurse is caring for (helping) the child.

5. Mwen bezwen yon famasi pou m' achete remèd la.
I need a pharmacy to buy the medicine.

Additional Medical Vocabulary

The following vocabulary is included to help the medical professional communicate with limited Creole language knowledge. These terms will be understood by all Haitian medical personnel, including orderlies and nurses' aides and by most patients in urban areas although not every term will be understood by all patients in rural areas.

A:		D:	
abrasion	fwote	daze, dazed	toudi
abstain (food)	pa manje	deceased	mouri
administer (give)	bay	dead	mouri
apply	pase	dehydrated	kò sèch, dezidrate
affliction	maladi	delusion	foli
AIDS, HIV	SIDA	denture	atelye, danti
ailing	malad	detach	detache
allergy	alèji	diabetes	dyabèt, sik
anesthetize	andòmi	diaphragm	dyafram
antibiotic	antibyotik	diarrhea	djare,dyare
antidote	antidòt, remèd kont pwazon	diet	rejim
appendicitis	apenndisit	digest	dijere, pase nan vant
artery, vein	venn	diphtheria	difteri
assist	asiste, ede	directions (instructions)	eksplikasyon
B:		disinfect	dezenfekte
basin	kivèt	disrobe	dezabiye
bedwetter	pisannit	dislocated	dejwente
belch	rann gaz, degobye	dizziness	toudisman, vètij, tèt vire
bellyache	vant fè mal	dosage, dose	dòz
bicarbonate	bikabonak	drain (v)	degoute
bite	kout dan (n), mode (v)	drainage	drenaj
bleeding	senyen	E:	
blow (hit)	kou	effect	efè
breathe	respire	electrocardiogram	kontwòl kè
bronchitis	bwonchit	emaciated	mèg
bruise	metri	enrich, enriched	anrichi
bug	ti bèt	epidemic	epidemi
bump	frape (v)	epistaxis (nosebleed)	nen senyen
bump on head	konkonm, bòs	exam	egzamen
C:		examine (doctor)	konsilte
cap (for bottle)	bouchon	exhaustion	kòkraz, fatig
care for	swen, okipe	expert	ekspè, spesyalis
careful (be careful)	veye, fè atansyon	F:	
centipede/millipede	annipye, milpye, milpat	fatigue	fatig, feblès
cervix	bouch matris	feeling	sansasyon
childbirth	akouchman	fracture	kase, fractire
cirrhosis	siwoz	frail	enfim
colic	kolik	G:	
collapse (v)	endispoze	gall bladder	fyèl
congestion	konjesyon, toufe	germ	mikwòb
consent	konsanti, dakò	gonorrhea	grantchalè
console	rekonfòte, bay kouraj	gout	lagout
critical (grave)	grav		

H:		listless	molas
hourly	chak inè de tan	loose	lache
hydrogen peroxide	dlo oksijene	loosen	lage, desere
hygiene	ijyèn	lotion	krèm, losyon
hypertension	tansyon, tansyon wo	lumpy	gen ti boul
hypotension	tansyon ba	M:	
hysteria	krizdenè	membrane	manbran
I:		meningitis	menenjit
immobile	san mouvman	menopause	menopòz
impossible	enposib	migraine	migrèn, tèt fè mal
improvement	alemye, miyò	mixture	melanj
improvement	amelyorasyon, pwogrè	molar	dan dèyè
incisor	dan devan	motionless	san mouvman
incurable	san gerizon, engerisab	mouthwash	dezenfektan pou bouch
inebriated	sou, gri	muscle	misk , chè
infected	enfekte	muscular	miskle, manbre
infection	enfeksyon	N:	
inflammation	anflamasyon	nausea	gen vomisman
influenza	gwo grip	nervous	ajite, enève
injury	blese, domaj	nervousness	ajitasyon, enèvyman
insomnia	paka dòmi	newborn	nouvone, fèk fèt
inspect	enspekte, kontwole	nosebleed	nen senyen
inspection	enspeksyon	nostril	twou nen, narin
instruct	enstwi, montre	nourishing	nourisan
instruction	ansèyman	O:	
invalid	malad	obstruction	angòje, bouche
iodine	yòd, tentidyòd	occupation	okipasyon, metye
irritable	rechiya	operate on	fè operasyon, opere sou
irritated	eksite, irite	optician	optisyen
isolated	izole	organ	ògan, pati
J:		orthopedist	òtopedis
jaw	machwè	ovary	ovè
jaundice	lajònis	overdose	twòp remèd
jellyfish	lagratèl	overdue	anreta
joint	jwenti	overnight	pase nwit
K:		overweight	twò gwa
keep an eye on	voye je sou	ovulation	ovilasyon
kidney	ren	oxygen	oksijèn
kidney stone	pyè nan ren	P:	
knock out	blayi, degrennen	p.m.	apremidi 12-6, diswa 7-12
knuckle	jwenti dwèt	painful	fè mal
L:		painkiller	kalman, remèd pou doulè
laboratory	laboratwa	painless	san penn, san doulè
laceration	blese	palpitate	bat
latrine	latrin, watè	palpitation	palpitasyon, batman
lessen	bese	pancreas	pankre
let (permit)	kite, pèmèt	panic	panic, panike (v)
lethal	mòtel	paralyze	paralize
lethargic	fèb, manfouben	parasite	parazit
pathology	patoloji	pediatrician	pedyat, doktè timoun

payment	peyman	pee (urinate)	fè pipi, irinen, pise
penicillin	penisilin	rheumatism	rimatis
personal	prive	rhythm	kadans
perspiration	swe	rickets	rachitis
pharmacist	famasyen	right-handed	dwatye
phobia	lapè, laperèz	rigid	rijid, rèd
plastic surgery	chiriji estetik	ringworm	lateng
posture	posti, kanpe	rock (v)	baskile, balanse
powerful	fò, pisan	roll over	vire sou lòt bò
premature	avan lè, prematire	routine	woutin
premenstrual	anvan règ	**S:**	
prenatal	avan nesans	safely	byen, san malè
pressure	presyon	sanatorium	sanatoryòm
preventable	evitab	sane	sèn, gen bon tèt
probably	siman	save (keep)	sere
procedure	pwosede	scabies	gal
prolong	pwolonje, lonje	scald	chode
prostate	glann pwostat	scream	rèl, rele (v), kriye (v)
psychiatric	sikyatrik	scrotum	sak grenn
psychiatrist	sikyat	scrub	foubi
pulmonary	pilmonè, nan poumon	seizure	kriz
pulse	poul, batmankè	seriously	seryezman
purify	pirifye, dezenfekte	severely	grav
pus	pi	severety	severite
Q:		sex m/f	sèks
quarantine	karantèn	sex (have sex)	fè baygay, kouche
quickly	vit, byen vit	sickness	maladi
quiet	trankil, san bri	sinus	sinis
R:		sleep with	kouche ak
rabies	raj, laraj	sleeping	nan dòmi
radiation	reyonnman	sleepy	gen dòmi nan je
radiograph (v)	radyografye, fè radyografi	smallpox	vèrèt
rash, heat rash	gratèl, chofi	smelly	santi
reaction	reyaksyon	sore throat, laryngitis	gòj fè mal, anwe
reassure	rasire	sperm	dechay, jèm
recline	kouche	spine	rèl do
records (file)	dosye, dokiman	spleen	larat
rectum	rektòm, twou dèyè	spot	tach
reddened	wouji	sprain	antòs
refill (v)	replen	stammer	bege
reflex	reflèks	sternum	biskèt
refusal	refi	stomachache	vant fè mal
relapse	tonbe malad ankò	suddenly	sibitman, briskeman
relationship	relasyon	suffer	soufri
release (from hospital)	bay egzeyat	suffering	soufrans
relief	soulajman	suffocate (v)	toufe
respiration	respirasyon, souf	suffocation	etoufman
respond	reponn	survive	siviv, pase
rest (relax)	poze		

English	Creole	English	Creole
T:		ureter	irèt, kanal marasa
tablespoon	gwo kiyè	urgency, emergency	ijans
take off clothes	dezabiye	use (v)	sèvi
technique	teknik	**V:**	
tenderness	tandrès	vagina	bòbòt, vajin
tepid	tyèd	vaginal discharge	pèt blanch
term	tèm, limit	vague	vag
therapy	trètman	vaporizer	vaporizatè
thermometer	tèmomèt	variable	chanje, varyab
thorax	pwatrin, lestomak	varicose vein	varies
throb	bat	vegetative	vejetatif, sans konensans
throw up	rejte, vomi	vein, artery	venn
thrush	chit	venereal	veneryèn
tibia	zo janm	venom	pwazon
ticklish	sansib	ventilate	ayere, vante
tingling	pikotman	ventricle	vantrikil
tinnitus	tande bri nan zòrèy	vertebra	vètèb, zo do
tiredness	fatig	vertigo	vètij, tèt vire
toilet	watè, latrin	violence	vyolans
topical	remèd po	virgin	vyèj, ti fi
touth	dan	virus	viris
toxicity	toksisite	vision good/bad	wè byen / wè mal
train (v)	montre, antrene	visitor	vizitè
tranquilizer	kalman, trankilizan	visual	vizyèl
transfer	transfere	vital	enpòtan, vital
transfuse	bay san	vocal chord	kòd vokal
transfusion	transfizyon	vomiting	vomisman
transmissible	transmisib	vulva	pati fi, bouboun
transmission	transmisyon	**W:**	
treatable	ki kapab trete	waist	tay, senti
triceps	trisèp, misk dèyè ponyèt	ward (surgical)	sal chiriji
trimester	trimès, chak twa mwa	warm	tyèd (adj), chofe (v)
turn around	virewon	warmth	chalè
twisted	tòde, kokobe	warning	avètisman
U:		wart	vèri
ulcer	ilsè	watch over	veye
uncap	ouvri	weight loss	pèdi pwa
unclothed	dezabiye	wet nurse	nouris
uncommon	ra	womb	matris
uncooked	kri, san kwit	wonderful	mèvèye
uncross	dekwaze	**X:**	
underarm	anba bra	x-ray	radyografi
underdeveloped	soudevlope, rasi (child)	**Y:**	
undernourished	malnouri	yawn	baye
underweight	mèg, pa peze ase	yaws	pyan
undigested	pa dijere	you are welcome	padkwa, ou merite
uneducated	malapri	yourself	ou menm
unhealthy	malsen		
upper part	anlè		

About the author

Betty Turnbull earned her degree in education from Rockford College in 1970. With her husband, Wally, she served as a missionary in education and self-help development with the Baptist Haiti Mission from 1972 to 2002.

During her 30 years of service in Haiti, Turnbull developed the first rural preschool program which, today, has expanded into hundreds of schools across that nation, following the model she established.

The Mountain Maid Self Help Project Turnbull helped establish continues to provide training and income to over a thousand families in the mountains of Haiti.

Turnbull received an award of distinction from Rockford College in 1983 for her development and education work.

The author and her husband currently reside in Durham, NC. They have three children all of whom were born and raised in Haiti.

Notes

Notes

Notes

Notes

Notes